CONTENTS

Understanding the Lectionary	2
Making Choices in *Common Worship*	4
Book of Common Prayer	5
Certain Days and Occasions Commonly Observed	5
Key to Liturgical Colours	6
Principal Feasts, Holy Days and Festivals	6
Lesser Festivals and Commemorations	6
Lesser Festivals and Commemorations not observed in 2017–18	7
Common Worship	7
Book of Common Prayer	8
The Common of the Saints	9
Special Occasions	10
The *Common Worship* Calendar and Lectionary (including the Book of Common Prayer Calendar and Lectionary)	12
The *Common Worship* Additional Weekday Lectionary	92
Calendar 2018	96
Calendar 2019	96

D1081077

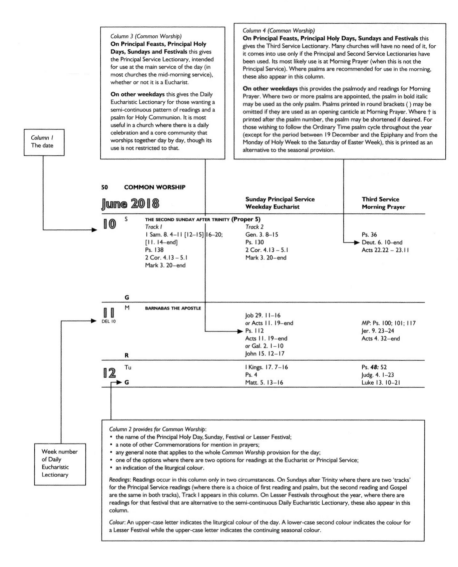

Column 1
The date

Column 3 (Common Worship)
On Principal Feasts, Principal Holy Days, Sundays and Festivals this gives the Principal Service Lectionary, intended for use at the main service of the day (in most churches the mid-morning service), whether or not it is a Eucharist.

On other weekdays this gives the Daily Eucharistic Lectionary for those wanting a semi-continuous pattern of readings and a psalm for Holy Communion. It is most useful in a church where there is a daily celebration and a core community that worships together day by day, though its use is not restricted to that.

Column 4 (Common Worship)
On Principal Feasts, Principal Holy Days, Sundays and Festivals this gives the Third Service Lectionary. Many churches will have no need of it, for it comes into use only if the Principal and Second Service Lectionaries have been used. Its most likely use is at Morning Prayer (when this is not the Principal Service). Where psalms are recommended for use in the morning, these also appear in this column.

On other weekdays this provides the psalmody and readings for Morning Prayer. Where two or more psalms are appointed, the psalm in bold italic may be used as the only psalm. Psalms printed in round brackets ( ) may be omitted if they are used as an opening canticle at Morning Prayer. Where † is printed after the psalm number, the psalm may be shortened if desired. For those wishing to follow the Ordinary Time psalm cycle throughout the year (except for the period between 19 December and the Epiphany and from the Monday of Holy Week to the Saturday of Easter Week), this is printed as an alternative to the seasonal provision.

50 COMMON WORSHIP		Sunday Principal Service	Third Service
June 2018		Weekday Eucharist	Morning Prayer
10 S	THE SECOND SUNDAY AFTER TRINITY **(Proper 5)**		
	Track 1	*Track 2*	
	1 Sam. 8. 4–11 [12–15] 16–20;	Gen. 3. 8–15	Ps. 36
	[11. 14–end]	Ps. 130	Deut. 6. 10–end
	Ps. 138	2 Cor. 4.13 – 5.1	Acts 22.22 – 23.11
	2 Cor. 4.13 – 5.1	Mark 3. 20–end	
	Mark 3. 20–end		
G			
11 M	BARNABAS THE APOSTLE		
DEL 10		Job 29. 11–16	MP: Ps. 100; 101; 117
		or Acts 11. 19–end	Jer. 9. 23–24
		Ps. 112	Acts 4. 32–end
		Acts 11. 19–end	
		or Gal. 2. 1–10	
R		John 15. 12–17	
12 Tu		1 Kings. 17. 7–16	Ps. *48*: 52
		Ps. 4	Judg. 4. 1–23
G		Matt. 5. 13–16	Luke 13. 10–21

Week number of Daily Eucharistic Lectionary

Column 2 provides for Common Worship:
• the name of the Principal Holy Day, Sunday, Festival or Lesser Festival;
• a note of other Commemorations for mention in prayers;
• any general note that applies to the whole *Common Worship* provision for the day;
• one of the options where there are two options for readings at the Eucharist or Principal Service;
• an indication of the liturgical colour.

Readings: Readings occur in this column only in two circumstances. On Sundays after Trinity where there are two 'tracks' for the Principal Service readings (where there is a choice of first reading and psalm, but the second reading and Gospel are the same in both tracks), Track I appears in this column. On Lesser Festivals throughout the year, where there are readings for that festival that are alternative to the semi-continuous Daily Eucharistic Lectionary, these also appear in this column.

Colour: An upper-case letter indicates the liturgical colour of the day. A lower-case second colour indicates the colour for a Lesser Festival while the upper-case letter indicates the continuing seasonal colour.

LECTIONARY

Column 5 (Common Worship)
On Principal Feasts, Principal Holy Days, Sundays and Festivals this gives the Second Service Lectionary, intended for use when a second set of readings is required. Its most likely use is in the evening, when the Principal Service Lectionary has been used in the morning. Sometimes it might be used at an evening Eucharist. Where the second reading is not a Gospel reading, an alternative to meet this need is provided. Where psalms are recommended for use in the evening, these also appear in this column.

On other weekdays this provides the psalmody and readings for Evening Prayer. Where two or more psalms are provided, the psalm in bold italic may be used as the only psalm. Psalms printed in round brackets ( ) may be omitted if they are used as an opening canticle at Evening Prayer. Where † is printed after the psalm number, the psalm may be shortened if desired. For those wishing to follow the Ordinary Time psalm cycle throughout the year (except for the period between 19 December and the Epiphany and from the Monday of Holy Week to the Saturday of Easter Week), this is printed as an alternative to the seasonal provision.

Column 7 (Book of Common Prayer)
This provides the readings for Morning Prayer, together with psalm provision where it varies from the BCP monthly cycle.

A letter to indicate liturgical colour in this column indicates a change of colour before Evening Prayer. The symbol in bold lower case, **ct**, indicates that the Collect at Evening Prayer should be that of the following day.

BOOK OF COMMON PRAYER

Second Service Evening Prayer	Calendar and Holy Communion	Morning Prayer	Evening Prayer
	THE SECOND SUNDAY AFTER TRINITY		
Ps. 37. 1–17 (or 37. 1–11)	Gen. 12. 1–4	Ps. 36	Ps. 37. 1–17
Jer. 6. 16–21	Ps. 120	Deut. 6. 10–end	(or 37. 1–11)
Rom. 9. 1–13	1 John 3. 13–end	Acts 22.22–23.11	Jer. 6. 16–21
Gospel: Luke 7. 11–17	Luke 14. 16–24		Rom. 9. 1–13
or First EP of Barnabas			*or First EP of Barnabas*
Ps. 1; 15			Ps. 1; 15
Isa. 42. 5–12			Isa. 42. 5–12
Acts 14. 8–end			Acts 14. 8–end
R ct	G		**R ct**
	BARNABAS THE APOSTLE		
EP: Ps. 147	Job 29. 11–16	(Ps. 100; 101; 117)	(Ps. 147)
Eccles. 12. 9–end	Ps. 112	Jer. 9. 23–24	Eccles. 12. 9–end
or Tobit 4. 5–11	Acts 11. 22–end	Acts 4. 32–end	*or* Tobit 4. 5–11
Acts 9. 26–31	John 15. 12–16		Acts 9. 26–31
	R		
Ps. 50		Judg. 4. 1–23	Ezra ch. 3
Ezra ch. 3		Luke 13. 10–21	Rom. 9. 19–end
Rom. 9. 19–end	G		

A letter to indicate liturgical colour in this column indicates a change of colour before Evening Prayer. The symbol in bold lower case, **ct**, indicates that the Collect at Evening Prayer should be that of the following day.

Column 6 provides for Book of Common Prayer:
• the name of the Principal Holy Day, Sunday, Festival or Lesser Festival;
• any general note that applies to the whole Prayer Book provision for the day and an indication of points at which users may wish to draw on *Common Worship* material on the opposite page where the BCP has no provision;
• the Lectionary for the Eucharist on any day for which provision is made;
• an indication of liturgical colour (see column 2).

Column 8 (Book of Common Prayer)
This provides the readings for Evening Prayer, together with psalm provision where it varies from the BCP monthly cycle.

Making Choices in *Common Worship*

Common Worship makes provision for a variety of pastoral and liturgical circumstances. It needs to, for it has to serve some church communities where Morning Prayer, Holy Communion and Evening Prayer are all celebrated every day, and yet be useful also in a church with only one service a week, and that service varying in form and time from week to week.

At the beginning of the year, some decisions in principle need to be taken.

In relation to the Calendar, a decision needs to be taken whether to keep The Epiphany on Saturday 6 January or on Sunday 7 January, whether to keep The Presentation of Christ (Candlemas) on Friday 2 February or on Sunday 28 January, and whether to keep the Feast of All Saints on Thursday 1 November or on Sunday 4 November.

In relation to the Lectionary, the initial choices every year to decide in relation to Sundays are:

- which of the services on a Principal Feast, Principal Holy Day, Sunday or Festival constitutes the 'Principal Service'; then use the Principal Service Lectionary (column 3) consistently for that service through the year;
- during the Sundays after Trinity, whether to use Track 1 of the Principal Service Lectionary (column 2), where the first reading stays over several weeks with one Old Testament book read semi-continuously, or Track 2 (column 3), where the first reading is chosen for its relationship to the Gospel reading of the day;
- which, if any, service on a Principal Feast, Principal Holy Day, Sunday or Festival constitutes the 'Second Service'; then use the Second Service Lectionary (column 5) consistently for that service through the year;
- which, if any, service on a Principal Feast, Principal Holy Day, Sunday or Festival constitutes the 'Third Service'; then use the Third Service Lectionary (column 4) consistently for that service through the year.

And in relation to weekdays:

- whether to use the Daily Eucharistic Lectionary (column 3) consistently for weekday celebrations of Holy Communion (with the exception of Principal Feasts, Principal Holy Days and Festivals) or to make some use of the Lesser Festival provision;
- whether to follow the first psalm provision in column 4 (morning) and column 5 (evening), where psalms during the seasons have a seasonal flavour but in ordinary time follow a sequential pattern; or to follow the alternative provision in the same columns, where psalms follow the sequential pattern throughout the year, except for the period between 19 December and The Epiphany and from the Monday of Holy Week to the Saturday of Easter Week; or to follow the psalm cycle in the Book of Common Prayer, where they are nearly always used 'in course';
- whether to use the Additional Weekday Lectionary (which begins on page 92) for weekday services (other than Holy Communion). It provides a one-year cycle of two readings for each day (except for Sundays, Principal Feasts, Principal Holy Days, Festivals and during Holy Week). Since each of the readings is designed to 'stand alone' (that is, it is complete in itself and will make sense to the worshipper who has not attended on the previous day and who will not be present on the next day), it is intended particularly for use in those churches and cathedrals that attract occasional rather than regular congregations.

The flexibility of *Common Worship* is intended to enable the church and the minister to find the most helpful provision for them. But once a decision is made, it is advisable to stay with that decision through the year or at the very least through a complete season.

All Bible references (except to the psalms) are to the New Revised Standard Version, Anglicized edition (1995). Those who use other Bible translations should check the verse numbers against the NRSV. References to the psalms are to the *Common Worship* Psalter.

Book of Common Prayer

A separate Lectionary for the Book of Common Prayer is no longer issued. Provision is made on the right-hand pages of this Lectionary for BCP worship on all Sundays in the year, for the major festivals and for Morning and Evening Prayer. The Epistles and Gospels for Holy Communion are those of 1662, with the additions and variations of 1928, now authorized under the *Common Worship* overall provision. The Old Testament readings and psalms for these services, formerly appended to the Series One Holy Communion service, may be used but are not mandatory with the 1662 order.

Readings for Morning and Evening Prayer, which are the same as those for *Common Worship*, are set out in the BCP section for Sundays and weekdays. The special psalm provision of the BCP is given; however, where the *Common Worship* psalm provision is used, verse numbering may occasionally differ slightly from that in the BCP Psalter, and appropriate adjustment will have to be made (a table of variations in verse numbering can be found at www.churchofengland.org/prayer-worship/worship/texts/daily2/psalter/psalterverses.aspx). Otherwise the Psalter is read in course daily through each month.

The Calendar observes BCP dates when these differ from those of *Common Worship*; for example, St Thomas on 21 December. Additional commemorations in the *Common Worship* Calendar are not included, but those who wish to observe them may use the *Collects and Post Communions in Traditional Language: Lesser Festivals, Common of the Saints, Special Occasions* (Church House Publishing).

The Lectionaries of 1871 and 1922, to be found in many copies of the BCP, are still authorized and may be used, but – with the exception of the psalms and readings for Holy Communion mentioned above – the Additional Alternative Lectionary (1961) is no longer authorized for public worship.

Although those who use the BCP, for private or public worship or both, are free to follow any of the authorized lectionaries, there is much to be said for common usage across the Church of England, so that the same passages are being read by all. It is of course appropriate that BCP readings should be taken from the Authorized or King James Version for harmony of style, with the daily recitation of the BCP Psalter.

The integrity of the BCP as the traditional source of worship in the Church of England is not in any way affected by the use of a common lectionary for the daily offices.

CERTAIN DAYS AND OCCASIONS COMMONLY OBSERVED

Plough Sunday may be observed on 7 January 2018.

The Week of Prayer for Christian Unity may be observed from 18 to 25 January 2018.

Education Sunday may be observed on 9 September 2018.

Rogation Sunday may be observed on 6 May 2018.

The Feast of Dedication is observed on the anniversary of the dedication or consecration of a church, or, when the actual date is unknown, on 7 October 2018. In CW, 28 October 2018 is an alternative date.

Ember Days. CW encourages the bishop to set the Ember Days in each diocese in the week before the ordinations, whereas in BCP the dates are fixed.

Days of Discipline and Self-Denial in CW are the weekdays of Lent and all Fridays in the year, except all Principal Feasts and festivals outside Lent and Fridays between Easter Day and Pentecost. The eves of Principal Feasts are also appropriately kept as days of discipline and self-denial in preparation for the feast.

Days of Fasting and Abstinence according to the BCP are the forty days of Lent, the Ember Days at the four seasons, the three Rogation Days, and all Fridays in the year except Christmas Day. The BCP also orders the observance of the Evens or Vigils before The Nativity of our Lord, The Purification of the Blessed Virgin Mary, The Annunciation of the Blessed Virgin Mary, Easter Day, Ascension Day, Pentecost, and before the following saints' days: Matthias, John the Baptist, Peter, James, Bartholomew, Matthew, Simon and Jude, Andrew, Thomas, and All Saints. (If any of these days falls on Monday, the Vigil is to be kept on the previous Saturday.)

KEY TO LITURGICAL COLOURS

Common Worship suggests appropriate liturgical colours. They are not mandatory, and traditional or local use may be followed.

For a detailed discussion of when colours may be used, see *Common Worship: Services and Prayers for the Church of England* (Church House Publishing), *New Handbook of Pastoral Liturgy* (SPCK) or *A Companion to Common Worship: Volume I* (SPCK).

W White
𝖂 Gold or white
R Red
P Purple (may vary from 'Roman purple' to violet, with blue as an alternative; a Lent array of sackcloth may be used in Lent, and rose pink on The Third Sunday of Advent and Fourth Sunday of Lent)
G Green

When a lower-case letter accompanies an upper-case letter, the lower-case letter indicates the liturgical colour appropriate to the Lesser Festival of that day, while the upper-case letter indicates the continuing seasonal colour.

PRINCIPAL FEASTS, HOLY DAYS AND FESTIVALS

Principal Feasts, and other Principal Holy Days (Ash Wednesday, Maundy Thursday, Good Friday) are printed in **LARGE BOLD CAPITALS** in the Lectionary.

There are no longer proper readings relating to the Holy Spirit on the six days after Pentecost. Instead they have been located on the nine days before Pentecost.

When Patronal and Dedication Festivals are kept as Principal Feasts, they may be transferred to the nearest Sunday, unless that day is already either a Principal Feast or The First Sunday of Advent, The Baptism of Christ, The First Sunday of Lent or Palm Sunday.

Festivals are printed in the Lectionary in SMALL BOLD CAPITALS.

For each day there is a full liturgical provision for the Holy Communion and for Morning and Evening Prayer. Most holy days that are in the category 'Festival' are provided with an optional First Evening Prayer. Its use is entirely at the discretion of the minister. Where it is used, the liturgical colour for the next day should be used at that First Evening Prayer, and this has been indicated in the provision on the following pages.

LESSER FESTIVALS AND COMMEMORATIONS

Lesser Festivals (printed in **bold roman** typeface) are observed at the level appropriate to a particular church. The readings and psalms for The Common of the Saints are listed on page 9. In addition, there are special readings appropriate to the Festival listed in the first column. The daily psalms and readings at Morning and Evening Prayer are not usually superseded by those for Lesser Festivals, but the readings and psalms for Holy Communion may on occasion be used at Morning or Evening Prayer.

Commemorations are printed in the Lectionary in *italic* typeface. They do not have collect, psalm or readings, but may be observed by mention in prayers of intercession and thanksgiving. For local reasons, or where there is an established tradition in the wider Church, they may be kept as Lesser Festivals using the appropriate material from The Common of the Saints. Equally, it may be desirable to observe some Lesser Festivals as Commemorations.

If a Lesser Festival or a Commemoration falls on a Principal Feast, Principal Holy Day, Sunday or Festival, it is not normally observed that year, although it may be celebrated, where there is sufficient reason, on the nearest available day. Lesser Festivals and Commemorations which, for this reason, would not be celebrated in 2017–18 are listed on pages 7–8, so that, if desired, they may be mentioned in prayers of intercession and thanksgiving.

LESSER FESTIVALS AND COMMEMORATIONS NOT OBSERVED IN 2017–18

The Lesser Festivals and Commemorations (shown in italics) listed below fall on a Sunday or during Holy Week or Easter Week this year, and are thus not observed in this Lectionary.

Common Worship

2017

December

3	*Francis Xavier, Missionary, Apostle of the Indies, 1552*
17	*Eglantyne Jebb, Social Reformer, Founder of 'Save the Children', 1928*
31	*John Wyclif, Reformer, 1384*

2018

January

21	Agnes, Child Martyr at Rome, 304
28	Thomas Aquinas, Priest, Philosopher, Teacher, 1274

February

4	*Gilbert of Sempringham, Founder of the Gilbertine Order, 1189*
14	Cyril and Methodius, Missionaries to the Slavs, 869 and 885
	Valentine, Martyr at Rome, c. 269

March

18	*Cyril, Bishop of Jerusalem, Teacher, 386*
26	*Harriet Monsell, Founder of the Community of St John the Baptist, Clewer, 1883*
31	*John Donne, Priest, Poet, 1631*

April

1	*Frederick Denison Maurice, Priest, Teacher, 1872*
9	*Dietrich Bonhoeffer, Lutheran Pastor, Martyr, 1945*
29	Catherine of Siena, Teacher, 1380

May

20	Alcuin of York, Deacon, Abbot of Tours, 804

June

3	*The Martyrs of Uganda, 1885–87 and 1977*
17	*Samuel and Henrietta Barnett, Social Reformers, 1913 and 1936*

July

1	*Henry, John and Henry Venn the Younger, Priests, Evangelical Divines, 1797, 1813 and 1873*
15	Swithun, Bishop of Winchester, c. 862
	Bonaventure, Friar, Bishop, Teacher, 1274
29	Mary, Martha and Lazarus, Companions of Our Lord

August

5	Oswald, King of Northumbria, Martyr, 642

September

2	*The Martyrs of Papua New Guinea, 1901 and 1942*
9	*Charles Fuge Lowder, Priest, 1880*

16	Ninian, Bishop of Galloway, Apostle of the Picts, *c.* 432
	Edward Bouverie Pusey, Priest, Tractarian, 1882
30	*Jerome, Translator of the Scriptures, Teacher, 420*

November

11	Martin, Bishop of Tours, *c.* 397
18	Elizabeth of Hungary, Princess of Thuringia, Philanthropist, 1231
25	*Catherine of Alexandria, Martyr, 4th century*
	Isaac Watts, Hymn Writer, 1748

Book of Common Prayer

2017

December

31	Silvester, Bishop of Rome, 335

2018

January
21	Agnes, Child Martyr at Rome, 304

February
14	Valentine, Martyr at Rome, *c.* 269

March
18	Edward, King of the West Saxons, 978

April
3	Richard, Bishop of Chichester, 1253
4	Ambrose, Bishop of Milan, 397

May
6	John the Evangelist, ante Portam Latinam
27	The Venerable Bede, Monk at Jarrow, Scholar, Historian, 735

June
17	Alban, first Martyr of Britain, *c.* 250

July
15	Swithun, Bishop of Winchester, *c.* 862

September
30	Jerome, Translator of the Scriptures, Teacher, 420

November
11	Martin, Bishop of Tours, *c.* 397
25	Catherine of Alexandria, Martyr, 4th century

THE COMMON OF THE SAINTS

The Blessed Virgin Mary

Genesis 3. 8–15, 20; Isaiah 7. 10–14; Micah 5. 1–4

Psalms 45. 10–17; 113; 131

Acts 1. 12–14; Romans 8. 18–30; Galatians 4. 4–7

Luke 1. 26–38; Luke 1. 39–47; John 19. 25–27

Martyrs

2 Chronicles 24. 17–21; Isaiah 43. 1–7; Jeremiah 11. 18–20; Wisdom 4. 10–15

Psalms 3; 11; 31. 1–5; 44. 18–24; 126

Romans 8. 35–end; 2 Corinthians 4. 7–15; 2 Timothy 2. 3–7 [8–13]; Hebrews 11. 32–end; 1 Peter 4. 12–end; Revelation 12. 10–12a

Matthew 10. 16–22; Matthew 10. 28–39; Matthew 16. 24–26; John 12. 24–26; John 15. 18–21

Teachers of the Faith and Spiritual Writers

1 Kings 3. [6–10] 11–14; Proverbs 4. 1–9; Wisdom 7. 7–10, 15–16; Ecclesiasticus 39. 1–10

Psalms 19. 7–10; 34. 11–17; 37. 31–35; 119. 89–96; 119. 97–104

1 Corinthians 1. 18–25; 1 Corinthians 2. 1–10; 1 Corinthians 2. 9–end;

Ephesians 3. 8–12; 2 Timothy 4. 1–8; Titus 2. 1–8

Matthew 5. 13–19; Matthew 13. 52–end; Matthew 23. 8–12; Mark 4. 1–9; John 16. 12–15

Bishops and Other Pastors

1 Samuel 16. 1, 6–13; Isaiah 6. 1–8; Jeremiah 1. 4–10; Ezekiel 3. 16–21; Malachi 2. 5–7

Psalms 1; 15; 16. 5–end; 96; 110

Acts 20. 28–35; 1 Corinthians 4. 1–5; 2 Corinthians 4. 1–10 (or 1–2, 5–7); 2 Corinthians 5. 14–20; 1 Peter 5. 1–4

Matthew 11. 25–end; Matthew 24. 42–46; John 10. 11–16; John 15. 9–17; John 21. 15–17

Members of Religious Communities

1 Kings 19. 9–18; Proverbs 10. 27–end; Song of Solomon 8. 6–7; Isaiah 61.10 – 62.5; Hosea 2. 14–15, 19–20

Psalms 34. 1–8; 112. 1–9; 119. 57–64; 123; 131

Acts 4. 32–35; 2 Corinthians 10.17 – 11.2; Philippians 3. 7–14; 1 John 2. 15–17; Revelation 19. 1, 5–9

Matthew 11. 25–end; Matthew 19. 3–12; Matthew 19. 23–end; Luke 9. 57–end; Luke 12. 32–37

Missionaries

Isaiah 52. 7–10; Isaiah 61. 1–3a; Ezekiel 34. 11–16; Jonah 3. 1–5

Psalms 67; 87; 97; 100; 117

Acts 2. 14, 22–36; Acts 13. 46–49; Acts 16. 6–10; Acts 26. 19–23; Romans 15. 17–21; 2 Corinthians 5.11 – 6.2

Matthew 9. 35–end; Matthew 28. 16–end; Mark 16. 15–20; Luke 5. 1–11; Luke 10. 1–9

Any Saint

Genesis 12. 1–4; Proverbs 8. 1–11; Micah 6. 6–8; Ecclesiasticus 2. 7–13 [14–end]

Psalms 32; 33. 1–5; 119. 1–8; 139. 1–4 [5–12]; 145. 8–14

Ephesians 3. 14–19; Ephesians 6. 11–18; Hebrews 13. 7–8, 15–16; James 2. 14–17; 1 John 4. 7–16; Revelation 21. [1–4] 5–7

Matthew 19. 16–21; Matthew 25. 1–13; Matthew 25. 14–30; John 15. 1–8; John 17. 20–end

SPECIAL OCCASIONS

The Guidance of the Holy Spirit
Proverbs 24. 3–7; Isaiah 30. 15–21; Wisdom 9. 13–17
Psalms 25. 1–9; 104. 26–33; 143. 8–10
Acts 15. 23–29; Romans 8. 22–27; I Corinthians 12. 4–13
Luke 14. 27–33; John 14. 23–26; John 16. 13–15

The Commemoration of the Faithful Departed
Lamentations 3. 17–26, 31–33 or Wisdom 3. 1–9
Psalm 23 or Psalm 27. 1–6, 16–end
Romans 5. 5–11 or I Peter 1. 3–9
John 5. 19–25 or John 6. 37–40

Rogation Days
Deuteronomy 8. 1–10; I Kings 8. 35–40; Job 28. 1–11
Psalms 104. 21–30; 107. 1–9; 121
Philippians 4. 4–7; 2 Thessalonians 3. 6–13; I John 5. 12–15
Matthew 6. 1–15; Mark 11. 22–24; Luke 11. 5–13

Harvest Thanksgiving
Year A
Deuteronomy 8. 7–18 or Deuteronomy 28. 1–14
Psalm 65
2 Corinthians 9. 6–end
Luke 12. 16–30 or Luke 17. 11–19

Year B
Joel 2. 21–27
Psalm 126
I Timothy 2. 1–7 or I Timothy 6. 6–10
Matthew 6. 25–33

Year C
Deuteronomy 26. 1–11
Psalm 100
Philippians 4. 4–9 or Revelation 14. 14–18
John 6. 25–35

Mission and Evangelism
Isaiah 49. 1–6; Isaiah 52. 7–10; Micah 4. 1–5
Psalms 2; 46; 67
Acts 17. 12–end; 2 Corinthians 5.14 – 6.2; Ephesians 2. 13–end
Matthew 5. 13–16; Matthew 28. 16–end; John 17. 20–end

The Unity of the Church
Jeremiah 33. 6–9a; Ezekiel 36. 23–28; Zephaniah 3. 16–end
Psalms 100; 122; 133
Ephesians 4. 1–6; Colossians 3. 9–17; I John 4. 9–15
Matthew 18. 19–22; John 11. 45–52; John 17. 11b–23

The Peace of the World

Isaiah 9. 1–6; Isaiah 57. 15–19; Micah 4. 1–5

Psalms 40. 14–17; 72. 1–7; 85. 8–13

Philippians 4. 6–9; 1 Timothy 2. 1–6; James 3. 13–18

Matthew 5. 43–end; John 14. 23–29; John 15. 9–17

Social Justice and Responsibility

Isaiah 32. 15–end; Amos 5. 21–24; Amos 8. 4–7; Acts 5. 1–11

Psalms 31. 21–24; 85. 1–7; 146. 5–10

Colossians 3. 12–15; James 2. 1–4

Matthew 5. 1–12; Matthew 25. 31–end; Luke 16. 19–end

Ministry (including Ember Days)

Numbers 11. 16–17, 24–29; Numbers 27. 15–end; 1 Samuel 16. 1–13a

Isaiah 6. 1–8; Isaiah 61. 1–3; Jeremiah 1. 4–10

Psalms 40. 8–13; 84. 8–12; 89. 19–25; 101. 1–5, 7; 122

Acts 20. 28–35; 1 Corinthians 3. 3–11; Ephesians 4. 4–16; Philippians 3. 7–14

Luke 4. 16–21; Luke 12. 35–43; Luke 22. 24–27; John 4. 31–38; John 15. 5–17

In Time of Trouble

Genesis 9. 8–17; Job 1. 13–end; Isaiah 38. 6–11

Psalms 86. 1–7; 107. 4–15; 142. 1–7

Romans 3. 21–26; Romans 8. 18–25; 2 Corinthians 8. 1–5, 9

Mark 4. 35–end; Luke 12. 1–7; John 16. 31–end

For the Sovereign

Joshua 1. 1–9; Proverbs 8. 1–16

Psalms 20; 101; 121

Romans 13. 1–10; Revelation 21.22 – 22.4

Matthew 22. 16–22; Luke 22. 24–30

December 2017

				Sunday Principal Service / Weekday Eucharist	Third Service / Morning Prayer

3 S — **THE FIRST SUNDAY OF ADVENT**
CW Year B begins

Ist Sunday (handwritten)

P

Isa. 64. 1–9
Ps. 80. 1–8, 18–20 (or 80. 1–8)
1 Cor. 1. 3–9
Mark 13. 24–end

Ps. 44
Isa. 2. 1–5
Luke 12. 35–48

---

4 M — *John of Damascus, Monk, Teacher, c. 749; Nicholas Ferrar, Deacon, Founder of the Little Gidding Community, 1637*
Daily Eucharistic Lectionary Year 2 begins

P

Isa. 2. 1–5
Ps. 122
Matt. 8. 5–11

Ps. **50**; 54
alt. Ps. *1*; 2; 3
Isa. 25. 1–9
Matt. 12. 1–21

---

5 Tu

P

Isa. 11. 1–10
Ps. 72. 1–4, 18–19
Luke 10. 21–24

Ps. **80**; 82
alt. Ps. **5**; 6; (8)
Isa. 26. 1–13
Matt. 12. 22–37

---

6 W — **Nicholas, Bishop of Myra, c. 326**
Com. Bishop
also Isa. 61. 1–3
1 Tim. 6. 6–11
Pw Mark 10. 13–16

or Isa. 25. 6–10a
Ps. 23
Matt. 15. 29–37

Ps. 5; **7**
alt. Ps. 119. 1–32
Isa. 28. 1–13
Matt. 12. 38–end

---

7 Th — **Ambrose, Bishop of Milan, Teacher, 397**
Com. Teacher
also Isa. 41. 9b–13
Luke 22. 24–30
Pw

or Isa. 26. 1–6
Ps. 118. 18–27a
Matt. 7. 21, 24–27

Ps. **42**; 43
alt. Ps. 14; **15**; 16
Isa. 28. 14–end
Matt. 13. 1–23

---

8 F — **The Conception of the Blessed Virgin Mary**
Com. BVM
Pw

or Isa. 29. 17–end
Ps. 27. 1–4, 16–17
Matt. 9. 27–31

Ps. **25**; 26
alt. Ps. 17; **19**
Isa. 29. 1–14
Matt. 13. 24–43

---

9 Sa

P

Isa. 30. 19–21, 23–26
Ps. 146. 4–9
Matt. 9.35 – 10.1, 6–8

Ps. **9**; (10)
alt. Ps. 20; 21; **23**
Isa. 29. 15–end
Matt. 13. 44–end

---

10 S — **THE SECOND SUNDAY OF ADVENT**

P

Isa. 40. 1–11
Ps. 85. 1–2, 8–end
(*or* 85. 8–end)
2 Pet. 3. 8–15a
Mark 1. 1–8

Ps. 80
Baruch 5. 1–9
or Zeph. 3. 14–end
Luke 1. 5–20

---

11 M

P

Isa. ch. 35
Ps. 85. 7–end
Luke 5. 17–26

Ps. 44
alt. Ps. 27; **30**
Isa. 30. 1–18
Matt. 14. 1–12

---

12 Tu

P

Isa. 40. 1–11
Ps. 96. 1, 10–end
Matt. 18. 12–14

Ps. **56**; 57
alt. Ps. 32; **36**
Isa. 30. 19–end
Matt. 14. 13–end

---

13 W — **Lucy, Martyr at Syracuse, 304**
Ember Day*
Samuel Johnson, Moralist, 1784
Com. Martyr
also Wisd. 3. 1–7
2 Cor. 4. 6–15
Pr

or Isa. 40. 25–end
Ps. 103. 8–13
Matt. 11. 28–end

Ps. **62**; 63
alt. Ps. 34
Isa. ch. 31
Matt. 15. 1–20

---

14 Th — **John of the Cross, Poet, Teacher, 1591**
Com. Teacher
esp. 1 Cor. 2. 1–10
also John 14. 18–23
Pw

or Isa. 41. 13–20
Ps. 145. 1, 8–13
Matt. 11. 11–15

Ps. 53; **54**; 60
alt. Ps. 37†
Isa. ch. 32
Matt. 15. 21–28

---

*For Ember Day provision, see p. 11.

Second Service Evening Prayer	Calendar and Holy Communion	Morning Prayer	Evening Prayer
	THE FIRST SUNDAY IN ADVENT Advent 1 Collect until Christmas Eve		
Ps. 25 (or 25. 1–9) Isa. 1. 1–20 Matt. 21. 1–13	Mic. 4. 1–4, 6–7 Ps. 25. 1–9 Rom. 13. 8–14 **P** Matt. 21. 1–13	Ps. 44 Isa. 2. 1–5 Luke 12. 35–48	Ps. 9 Isa. 1. 1–20 Mark 13. 24–end
Ps. 70; **71** alt. Ps. 4; 7 Isa. 42. 18–end Rev. ch. 19	**P**	Isa. 25. 1–9 Matt. 12. 1–21	Isa. 42. 18–end Rev. ch. 19
Ps. **74**; 75 alt. Ps. **9**; 10† Isa. 43. 1–13 Rev. ch. 20	**P**	Isa. 26. 1–13 Matt. 12. 22–37	Isa. 43. 1–13 Rev. ch. 20
Ps. 76; **77** alt. Ps. **11**; 12; 13 Isa. 43. 14–end Rev. 21. 1–8	**Nicholas, Bishop of Myra, c. 326** Com. Bishop **Pw**	Isa. 28. 1–13 Matt. 12. 38–end	Isa. 43. 14–end Rev. 21. 1–8
Ps. **40**; 46 alt. Ps. 18† Isa. 44. 1–8 Rev. 21. 9–21	**P**	Isa. 28. 14–end Matt. 13. 1–23	Isa. 44. 1–8 Rev. 21. 9–21
Ps. 16; **17** alt. Ps. 22 Isa. 44. 9–23 Rev. 21.22 – 22.5	**The Conception of the Blessed Virgin Mary** Isa. 29. 1–14 Matt. 13. 24–43 **Pw**		Isa. 44. 9–23 Rev. 21.22 – 22.5
Ps. **27**; 28 alt. Ps. **24**; 25 Isa. 44.24 – 45.13 Rev. 22. 6–end ct	**P**	Isa. 29. 15–end Matt. 13. 44–end	Isa. 44.24 – 45.13 Rev. 22. 6–end ct
Ps. 40 (or 40. 12–end) 1 Kings 22. 1–28 Rom. 15. 4–13 Gospel: Matt. 11. 2–11	**THE SECOND SUNDAY IN ADVENT** 2 Kings 22. 8–10; 23. 1–3 Ps. 50. 1–6 Rom. 15. 4–13 **P** Luke 21. 25–33	Ps. 80 Baruch 5. 1–9 or Zeph. 3. 14–end Luke 1. 5–20	Ps. 40 (or 40. 12–end) 1 Kings 22. 1–28 2 Pet. 3. 8–15a
Ps. **144**; 146 alt. Ps. 26; **28**; 29 Isa. 45. 14–end 1 Thess. ch. 1	**P**	Isa. 30. 1–18 Matt. 14. 1–12	Isa. 45. 14–end 1 Thess. ch. 1
Ps. **11**; 12; 13 alt. Ps. 33 Isa. ch. 46 1 Thess. 2. 1–12	**P**	Isa. 30. 19–end Matt. 14. 13–end	Isa. ch. 46 1 Thess. 2. 1–12
Ps. **10**; 14 alt. Ps. 119. 33–56 Isa. ch. 47 1 Thess. 2. 13–end	**Lucy, Martyr at Syracuse, 304** Com. Virgin Martyr **Pr**	Isa. ch. 31 Matt. 15. 1–20	Isa. ch. 47 1 Thess. 2. 13–end
Ps. 73 alt. Ps. 39; **40** Isa. 48. 1–11 1 Thess. ch. 3	**P**	Isa. ch. 32 Matt. 15. 21–28	Isa. 48. 1–11 1 Thess. ch. 3

December 2017

			Sunday Principal Service Weekday Eucharist	Third Service Morning Prayer
15	F	Ember Day*		
			Isa. 48. 17–19 Ps. 1 Matt. 11. 16–19	Ps. 85; **86** alt. Ps. 31 Isa. 33. 1–22
	P			Matt. 15. 29–end
16	Sa	Ember Day*		
			Ecclus. 48. 1–4, 9–11 or 2 Kings 2. 9–12 Ps. 80. 1–4, 18–19 Matt. 17. 10–13	Ps. 145 alt. Ps. 41; **42**; 43 Isa. ch. 35
	P			Matt. 16. 1–12
17	S	THE THIRD SUNDAY OF ADVENT O Sapientia**		
			Isa. 61. 1–4, 8–end Ps. 126 or Canticle: Magnificat 1 Thess. 5. 16–24	Ps. 50. 1–6; 62 Isa. ch. 12 Luke 1. 57–66
	P		John 1. 6–8, 19–28	
18	M		Jer. 23. 5–8 Ps. 72. 1–2, 12–13, 18–end Matt. 1. 18–24	Ps. 40 alt. Ps. 44 Isa. 38. 1–8, 21–22
	P			Matt. 16. 13–end
19	Tu		Judg. 13. 2–7, 24–end Ps. 71. 3–8	Ps. 144; **146** Isa. 38. 9–20
	P		Luke 1. 5–25	Matt. 17. 1–13
20	W			
			Isa. 7. 10–14 Ps. 24. 1–6 Luke 1. 26–38	Ps. **46**; 95 Isa. ch. 39 Matt. 17. 14–21
	P			
21	Th	***		
			Zeph. 3. 14–18 Ps. 33. 1–4, 11–12, 20–end Luke 1. 39–45	Ps. **121**; 122; 123 Zeph. 1.1 – 2.3 Matt. 17. 22–end
	P			
22	F			
			1 Sam. 1. 24–end Ps. 113 Luke 1. 46–56	Ps. **124**; 125; 126; 127 Zeph. 3. 1–13 Matt. 18. 1–20
	P			
23	Sa			
			Mal. 3. 1–4; 4. 5–end Ps. 25. 3–9 Luke 1. 57–66	Ps. 128; 129; **130**; 131 Zeph. 3. 14–end Matt. 18. 21–end
	P			
24	S	THE FOURTH SUNDAY OF ADVENT CHRISTMAS EVE	2 Sam. 7. 1–11, 16 Canticle: Magnificat or Ps. 89. 1–4, 19–26 (or 1–8) Rom. 16. 25–end Luke 1. 26–38	Ps. 144 Isa. 7. 10–16 Rom. 1. 1–7
	P			

*For Ember Day provision, see p. 11.
**Evening Prayer readings from the Additional Weekday Lectionary (see p. 92) may be used from 17 to 23 December.
***Thomas the Apostle may be celebrated on 21 December instead of 3 July.

Second Service Evening Prayer	Calendar and Holy Communion		Morning Prayer	Evening Prayer
Ps. 82; **90** alt. Ps. 35 Isa. 48. 12–end 1 Thess. 4. 1–12		P	Isa. 33. 1–22 Matt. 15. 29–end	Isa. 48. 12–end 1 Thess. 4. 1–12
Ps. 93; **94** alt. Ps. 45; **46** Isa. 49. 1–13 1 Thess. 4. 13–end ct	O Sapientia	P	Isa. ch. 35 Matt. 16. 1–12	Isa. 49. 1–13 1 Thess. 4. 13–end ct
Ps. 68. 1–19 (or 68. 1–8) Mal. 3. 1–4; ch. 4 Phil. 4. 4–7 Gospel: Matt. 14. 1–12	**THE THIRD SUNDAY IN ADVENT** Isa. ch. 35 Ps. 80. 1–7 1 Cor. 4. 1–5 Matt. 11. 2–10	P	Ps. 62 Isa. ch. 12 Luke 1. 57–66	Ps. 68. 1–19 (or 68. 1–8) Mal. 3. 1–4; ch. 4 Matt. 14. 1–12
Ps. 25; **26** alt. Ps. **47**; 49 Isa. 49. 14–25 1 Thess. 5. 1–11		P	Isa. 38. 1–8, 21–22 Matt. 16. 13–end	Isa. 49. 14–25 1 Thess. 5. 1–11
Ps. 10; **57** Isa. ch. 50 1 Thess. 5. 12–end		P	Isa. 38. 9–20 Matt. 17. 1–13	Isa. ch. 50 1 Thess. 5. 12–end
Ps. **4**; 9 Isa. 51. 1–8 2 Thess. ch. 1	Ember Day Ember CEG	P	Isa. ch. 39 Matt. 17. 14–21	Isa. 51. 1–8 2 Thess. ch. 1 or First EP of Thomas the Apostle (Ps. 27) Isa. ch. 35 Heb. 10.35 – 11.1 R ct
Ps. 80; **84** Isa. 51. 9–16 2 Thess. ch. 2	**THOMAS THE APOSTLE** Job 42. 1–6 Ps. 139. 1–11 Eph. 2. 19–end John 20. 24–end	R	(Ps. 92; 146) 2 Sam. 15. 17–21 or Ecclus. ch. 2 John 11. 1–16	(Ps. 139) Hab. 2. 1–4 1 Pet. 1. 3–12
Ps. 24; **48** Isa. 51. 17–end 2 Thess. ch. 3	Ember Day Ember CEG	P	Zeph. 3. 1–13 Matt. 18. 1–20	Isa. 51. 17–end 2 Thess. ch. 3
Ps. 89. 1–37 Isa. 52. 1–12 Jude ct	Ember Day Ember CEG	P	Zeph. 3. 14–end Matt. 18. 21–end	Isa. 52. 1–12 Jude ct
Evening Prayer Ps. 85 Zech. ch. 2 Rev. 1. 1–8	**THE FOURTH SUNDAY IN ADVENT** **CHRISTMAS EVE** Collect (1) Christmas Eve (2) Advent 1 Isa. 40. 1–9 Ps. 145. 17–end Phil. 4. 4–7 John 1. 19–28	P	Ps. 144 Isa. 7. 10–16 Rom. 1. 1–7	Ps. 85 Zech. ch. 2 Rev. 1. 1–8

December 2017

Date	Day / Colour		Sunday Principal Service Weekday Eucharist	Third Service Morning Prayer
25	M 𝔚	**CHRISTMAS DAY** *Any of the following sets of readings may be used on the evening of Christmas Eve and on Christmas Day. Set III should be used at some service during the celebration.*	*I* Isa. 9. 2–7 Ps. 96 Titus 2. 11–14 Luke 2. 1–14 [15–20] *II* Isa. 62. 6–end Ps. 97 Titus 3. 4–7 Luke 2. [1–7] 8–20 *III* Isa. 52. 7–10 Ps. 98 Heb. 1. 1–4 [5–12] John 1. 1–14	*MP*: Ps. ***110***; 117 Isa. 62. 1–5 Matt. 1. 18–end
26	Tu **R**	STEPHEN, DEACON, FIRST MARTYR	2 Chron. 24. 20–22 *or* Acts 7. 51–end Ps. 119. 161–168 Acts 7. 51–end *or* Gal. 2. 16b–20 Matt. 10. 17–22	*MP*: Ps. ***13***; 31. 1–8; 150 Jer. 26. 12–15 Acts ch. 6
27	W **W**	JOHN, APOSTLE AND EVANGELIST	Exod. 33. 7–11a Ps. 117 1 John ch. 1 John 21. 19b–end	*MP*: Ps. ***21***; 147. 13–end Exod. 33. 12–end 1 John 2. 1–11
28	Th **R**	THE HOLY INNOCENTS	Jer. 31. 15–17 Ps. 124 1 Cor. 1. 26–29 Matt. 2. 13–18	*MP*: Ps. ***36***; 146 Baruch 4. 21–27 *or* Gen. 37. 13–20 Matt. 18. 1–10
29	F **Wr**	**Thomas Becket, Archbishop of Canterbury, Martyr, 1170*** Com. Martyr *or* *esp.* Matt. 10. 28–33 *also* Ecclus. 51. 1–8	1 John 2. 3–11 Ps. 96. 1–4 Luke 2. 22–35	Ps. ***19***; 20 Jonah ch. 1 Col. 1. 1–14
30	Sa **W**		1 John 2. 12–17 Ps. 96. 7–10 Luke 2. 36–40	Ps. 111; 112; ***113*** Jonah ch. 2 Col. 1. 15–23
31	S **W**	THE FIRST SUNDAY OF CHRISTMAS	Isa. 61.10 – 62.3 Ps. 148 (*or* 148. 7–end) Gal. 4. 4–7 Luke 2. 15–21	Ps. 105. 1–11 Isa. 63. 7–9 Eph. 3. 5–12

*Thomas Becket may be celebrated on 7 July instead of 29 December.

Second Service Evening Prayer		Calendar and Holy Communion	Morning Prayer	Evening Prayer
		CHRISTMAS DAY		
EP: Ps. 8		Isa. 9. 2–7	Ps. 110; 117	Ps. 8
Isa. 65. 17–25		Ps. 98	Isa. 62. 1–5	Isa. 65. 17–25
Phil. 2. 5–11		Heb. 1. 1–12	Matt. 1. 18–end	Phil. 2. 5–11
or Luke 2. 1–20		John 1. 1–14		or Luke 2. 1–20
if it has not been used at the				
principal service of the day				
	W			
		STEPHEN, DEACON, FIRST MARTYR		
EP: Ps. 57; **86**		Collect	(Ps. 13; 31. 1–8; 150)	(Ps. 57; 86)
Gen. 4. 1–10		(1) Stephen	Jer. 26. 12–15	Gen. 4. 1–10
Matt. 23. 34–end		(2) Christmas	Acts ch. 6	Matt. 10. 17–22
		2 Chron. 24. 20–22		
		Ps. 119. 161–168		
		Acts 7. 55–end		
	R	Matt. 23. 34–end		
		JOHN, APOSTLE AND EVANGELIST		
EP: Ps. 97		Collect	(Ps. 21; 147. 13–end)	(Ps. 97)
Isa. 6. 1–8		(1) John	Exod. 33. 7–11a	Isa. 6. 1–8
1 John 5. 1–12		(2) Christmas	1 John 2. 1–11	1 John 5. 1–12
		Exod. 33. 18–end		
		Ps. 92. 11–end		
		1 John ch. 1		
	W	John 21. 19b–end		
		THE HOLY INNOCENTS		
EP: Ps. 123; **128**		Collect	(Ps. 36; 146)	(Ps. 124; 128)
Isa. 49. 14–25		(1) Innocents	Baruch 4. 21–27	Isa. 49. 14–25
Mark 10. 13–16		(2) Christmas	or Gen. 37. 13–20	Mark 10. 13–16
		Jer. 31. 10–17	Matt. 18. 1–10	
		Ps. 123		
		Rev. 14. 1–5		
	R	Matt. 2. 13–18		
		CEG of Christmas		
Ps. 131; **132**			Jonah ch. 1	Isa. 57. 15–end
Isa. 57. 15–end			Col. 1. 1–14	John 1. 1–18
John 1. 1–18	W			
		CEG of Christmas		
Ps. **65**; 84			Jonah ch. 2	Isa. 59. 1–15a
Isa. 59. 1–15a			Col. 1. 15–23	John 1. 19–28
John 1. 19–28				
ct	W			ct
		THE SUNDAY AFTER CHRISTMAS DAY		
Ps. 132		Isa. 62. 10–12	Ps. 105. 1–11	Ps. 132
Isa. ch. 35		Ps. 45. 1–7	Isa. 63. 7–9	Isa. ch. 35
Col. 1. 9–20		Gal. 4. 1–7	Eph. 3. 5–12	1 John 1. 1–7
or Luke 2. 41–end		Matt. 1. 18–end		or First EP of The
or First EP of The				Circumcision of Christ
Naming of Jesus				Ps. 148
Ps. 148				Jer. 23. 1–6
Jer. 23. 1–6				Col. 2. 8–15
Col. 2. 8–15	W			

January 2018

			Sunday Principal Service Weekday Eucharist	Third Service Morning Prayer

1 | M | THE NAMING AND CIRCUMCISION OF JESUS

Num. 6. 22–end
Ps. 8
Gal. 4. 4–7
Luke 2. 15–21

MP: Ps. *103*; 150
Gen. 17. 1–13
Rom. 2. 17–end

W

---

2 | Tu | **Basil the Great and Gregory of Nazianzus, Bishops, Teachers, 379 and 389**
Seraphim, Monk of Sarov, Spiritual Guide, 1833; Vedanayagam Samuel Azariah, Bishop in South India,
Evangelist, 1945

Com. Teacher   *or*   1 John 2. 22–28   Ps. 18. 1–30
esp. 2 Tim. 4. 1–8   Ps. 98. 1–4   Ruth ch. 1
W | Matt. 5. 13–19   John 1. 19–28   Col. 2. 8–end

---

3 | W

1 John 2.29 – 3.6   Ps. *127*; 128; 131
Ps. 98. 2–7   Ruth ch. 2
W | John 1. 29–34   Col. 3. 1–11

---

4 | Th

1 John 3. 7–10   Ps. 89. 1–37
Ps. 98. 1, 8–end   Ruth ch. 3
W | John 1. 35–42   Col. 3.12 – 4.1

---

5 | F

1 John 3. 11–21   Ps. 8; *48*
Ps. 100   Ruth 4. 1–17
John 1. 43–end   Col. 4. 2–end

W

---

6 | Sa | **THE EPIPHANY**

Isa. 60. 1–6   *MP*: Ps. *132*; 113
Ps. 72. [1–9] 10–15   Jer. 31. 7–14
Eph. 3. 1–12   John 1. 29–34
Matt. 2. 1–12

𝖂

or, if The Epiphany is celebrated on 7 January:
1 John 5. 5–13   Ps. *99*; 147. 1–12
Ps. 147. 13–end   Baruch 1.15 – 2.10
Mark 1. 7–11   *or* Jer. 23. 1–8
W | Matt. 20. 1–16

---

7 | S | THE BAPTISM OF CHRIST (THE FIRST SUNDAY OF EPIPHANY)
(or transferred to 8 January if The Epiphany is celebrated today. For The Epiphany, see provision on 6 January.)
Gen. 1. 1–5   Ps. 89. 19–29
Ps. 29   1 Sam. 16. 1–3, 13
Acts 19. 1–7   John 1. 29–34
𝖂 | Mark 1. 4–11

---

8 | M | For The Baptism, see provision on 7 January.
DEL 1 | 1 Sam. 1. 1–8   Ps. *2*; 110
                               Ps. 116. 10–15   *alt.* Ps. 71
                               Mark 1. 14–20   Gen. 1. 1–19
W | Matt. 21. 1–17

---

9 | Tu

1 Sam. 1. 9–20   Ps. 8; *9*
Canticle: 1 Sam. 2. 1, 4–8   *alt.* Ps. 73
or Magnificat   Gen. 1.20 – 2.3
W | Mark 1. 21–28   Matt. 21. 18–32

---

10 | W | *William Laud, Archbishop of Canterbury, 1645*

1 Sam. 3. 1–10, 19–20   Ps. 19; *20*
Ps. 40. 1–4, 7–10   *alt.* Ps. 77
Mark 1. 29–39   Gen. 2. 4–end
W | Matt. 21. 33–end

Second Service Evening Prayer		Calendar and Holy Communion	Morning Prayer	Evening Prayer
		THE CIRCUMCISION OF CHRIST		
EP: Ps. 115		Additional collect	(Ps. 103; 150)	(Ps. 115)
Deut. 30. [1–10] 11–end		Gen. 17. 3b–10	Gen. 17. 1–13	Deut. 30. [1–10]
Acts 3. 1–16		Ps. 98	Rom. 2. 17–end	11–end
		Rom. 4. 8–13		Acts 3. 1–16
		or Eph. 2. 11–18		
	W	Luke 2. 15–21		
Ps. 45; **46**			Ruth ch. 1	Isa. 60. 1–12
Isa. 60. 1–12			Col. 2. 8–end	John 1. 35–42
John 1. 35–42	**W**			
Ps. **2**; 110			Ruth ch. 2	Isa. 60. 13–end
Isa. 60. 13–end			Col. 3. 1–11	John 1. 43–end
John 1. 43–end	**W**			
Ps. 85; **87**			Ruth ch. 3	Isa. ch. 61
Isa. ch. 61			Col. 3.12 – 4.1	John 2. 1–12
John 2. 1–12	**W**			
First EP of The Epiphany			Ruth 4. 1–17	*First EP of The Epiphany*
Ps. 96; **97**			Col. 4. 2–end	Ps. 96; 97
Isa. 49. 1–13				Isa. 49. 1–13
John 4. 7–26				John 4. 7–26
⅏ ct				
or, if The Epiphany is				
celebrated on 7 January:				
Ps. 96; **97**				
Isa. ch. 62				
John 2. 13–end	**W**			⅏ ct
		THE EPIPHANY		
EP: Ps. **98**; 100		Isa. 60. 1–9	Ps. 132; 113	Ps. 72; 98
Baruch 4.36 – 5.end		Ps. 100	Jer. 31. 7–14	Baruch 4.36 – 5.end
or Isa. 60. 1–9		Eph. 3. 1–12	John 1. 29–34	*or* Isa. 60. 1–9
John 2. 1–11		Matt. 2. 1–12		John 2. 1–11
First EP of The Epiphany				
Ps. 96; **97**				
Isa. 49. 1–13				
John 4. 7–26				
Ps. 118				
Isa. 63. 7–end				
1 John ch. 3				
⅏ ct	⅏			
		THE FIRST SUNDAY AFTER THE EPIPHANY		
		To celebrate The Baptism of Christ, see *Common Worship* provision.		
Ps. 46; 47		Zech. 8. 1–8	Ps. 89. 19–29	Ps. 46; 47
Isa. 42. 1–9		Ps. 72. 1–8	1 Sam. 16. 1–3, 13	Isa. 42. 1–9
Eph. 2. 1–10		Rom. 12. 1–5	John 1. 29–34	Eph. 2. 1–10
Gospel: Matt. 3. 13–end		Luke 2. 41–end		
	W *or* **G**			
Ps. **34**; 36		**Lucian, Priest and Martyr, 290**	Gen. 1. 1–19	Amos ch. 1
alt. Ps. **72**; 75		Com. Martyr	Matt. 21. 1–17	1 Cor. 1. 1–17
Amos ch. 1				
1 Cor. 1. 1–17	**Wr** *or* **Gr**			
Ps. **45**; 46			Gen. 1.20 – 2.3	Amos ch. 2
alt. Ps. 74			Matt. 21. 18–32	1 Cor. 1. 18–end
Amos ch. 2				
1 Cor. 1. 18–end	**W** *or* **G**			
Ps. **47**; 48			Gen. 2. 4–end	Amos ch. 3
alt. Ps. 119. 81–104			Matt. 21. 33–end	1 Cor. ch. 2
Amos ch. 3				
1 Cor. ch. 2	**W** *or* **G**			

January 2018

			Sunday Principal Service / Weekday Eucharist	Third Service / Morning Prayer

11 Th — *Mary Slessor, Missionary in West Africa, 1915*
			1 Sam. 4. 1–11	Ps. *21*; 24
			Ps. 44. 10–15, 24–25	alt. Ps. 78. 1–39†
			Mark 1. 40–end	Gen. ch. 3
	W			Matt. 22. 1–14

12 F — **Aelred of Hexham, Abbot of Rievaulx, 1167**
Benedict Biscop, Abbot of Wearmouth, Scholar, 689
		Com. Religious	or 1 Sam. 8. 4–7, 10–end	Ps. *67*; 72
		also Ecclus. 15. 1–6	Ps. 89. 15–18	alt. Ps. 55
			Mark 2. 1–12	Gen. 4. 1–16, 25–26
	W			Matt. 22. 15–33

13 Sa — **Hilary, Bishop of Poitiers, Teacher, 367**
Kentigern (Mungo), Missionary Bishop in Strathclyde and Cumbria, 603; George Fox, Founder of the Society of Friends (the Quakers), 1691
		Com. Teacher	or 1 Sam. 9. 1–4, 17–19; 10. 1a	Ps. 29; *33*
		also 1 John 2. 18–25	Ps. 21. 1–6	alt. Ps. *76*; 79
		John 8. 25–32	Mark 2. 13–17	Gen. 6. 1–10
	W			Matt. 22. 34–end

14 S — **THE SECOND SUNDAY OF EPIPHANY**
			1 Sam. 3. 1–10 [11–20]	Ps. 145. 1–12
			Ps. 139. 1–5, 12–18 (or 1–9)	Isa. 62. 1–5
			Rev. 5. 1–10	1 Cor. 6. 11–end
	W		John 1. 43–end	

15 M — *(DEL 2)*
			1 Sam. 15. 16–23	Ps. 145; *146*
			Ps. 50. 8–10, 16–17, 24	alt. Ps. *80*; 82
			Mark 2. 18–22	Gen. 6.11 – 7.10
	W			Matt. 24. 1–14

16 Tu
			1 Sam. 16. 1–13	Ps. *132*; 147. 1–12
			Ps. 89. 19–27	alt. Ps. 87; *89. 1–18*
			Mark 2. 23–end	Gen. 7. 11–end
	W			Matt. 24. 15–28

17 W — **Antony of Egypt, Hermit, Abbot, 356**
Charles Gore, Bishop, Founder of the Community of the Resurrection, 1932
		Com. Religious	or 1 Sam. 17. 32–33, 37, 40–51	Ps. *81*; 147. 13–end
		esp. Phil. 3. 7–14	Ps. 144. 1–2, 9–10	alt. Ps. 119. 105–128
		also Matt. 19. 16–26	Mark 3. 1–6	Gen. 8. 1–14
	W			Matt. 24. 29–end

18 Th — *Amy Carmichael, Founder of the Dohnavur Fellowship, Spiritual Writer, 1951*
The Week of Prayer for Christian Unity until 25 January
			1 Sam. 18. 6–9; 19. 1–7	Ps. *76*; 148
			Ps. 56. 1–2, 8–end	alt. Ps. 90; *92*
			Mark 3. 7–12	Gen. 8.15 – 9.7
	W			Matt. 25. 1–13

19 F — **Wulfstan, Bishop of Worcester, 1095**
		Com. Bishop	or 1 Sam. 24. 3–22a	Ps. *27*; 149
		esp. Matt. 24. 42–46	Ps. 57. 1–2, 8–end	alt. Ps. *88*; (95)
			Mark 3. 13–19	Gen. 9. 8–19
	W			Matt. 25. 14–30

20 Sa — *Richard Rolle of Hampole, Spiritual Writer, 1349*
			2 Sam. 1. 1–4, 11–12, 17–19, 23–end	Ps. *122*; 128; 150
				alt. Ps. 96; *97*; 100
			Ps. 80. 1–6	Gen. 11. 1–9
	W		Mark 3. 20–21	Matt. 25. 31–end

21 S — **THE THIRD SUNDAY OF EPIPHANY**
			Gen. 14. 17–20	Ps. 113
			Ps. 128	Jonah 3. 1–5, 10
			Rev. 19. 6–10	John 3. 16–21
	W		John 2. 1–11	

Second Service Evening Prayer	Calendar and Holy Communion	Morning Prayer	Evening Prayer
Ps. *61*; 65 *alt.* Ps. 78. 40–end† Amos ch. 4 1 Cor. ch. 3 **W** *or* **G**		Gen. ch. 3 Matt. 22. 1–14	Amos ch. 4 1 Cor. ch. 3
Ps. 68 *alt.* Ps. 69 Amos 5. 1–17 1 Cor. ch. 4 **W** *or* **G**		Gen. 4. 1–16, 25–26 Matt. 22. 15–33	Amos 5. 1–17 1 Cor. ch. 4
Ps. 84; *85* *alt.* Ps. 81; *84* Amos 5. 18–end 1 Cor. ch. 5 ct **W** *or* **Gw**	**Hilary, Bishop of Poitiers, Teacher, 367** Com. Doctor	Gen. 6. 1–10 Matt. 22. 34–end	Amos 5. 18–end 1 Cor. ch. 5 ct
Ps. 96 Isa. 60. 9–end Heb. 6.17 – 7.10 *Gospel:* Matt. 8. 5–13 **W** *or* **G**	**THE SECOND SUNDAY AFTER THE EPIPHANY** 2 Kings 4. 1–17 Ps. 107. 13–22 Rom. 12. 6–16a John 2. 1–11	Ps. 145. 1–12 Isa. 62. 1–5 1 Cor. 6. 11–end	Ps. 96 Isa. 60. 9–end Heb. 6.17 – 7.10
Ps. 71 *alt.* Ps. *85*; 86 Amos ch. 6 1 Cor. 6. 1–11 **W** *or* **G**		Gen. 6.11 – 7.10 Matt. 24. 1–14	Amos ch. 6 1 Cor. 6. 1–11
Ps. 89. 1–37 *alt.* Ps. 89. 19–end Amos ch. 7 1 Cor. 6. 12–end **W** *or* **G**		Gen. 7. 11–end Matt. 24. 15–28	Amos ch. 7 1 Cor. 6. 12–end
Ps. *97*; 98 *alt.* Ps. *91*; 93 Amos ch. 8 1 Cor. 7. 1–24 **W** *or* **G**		Gen. 8. 1–14 Matt. 24. 29–end	Amos ch. 8 1 Cor. 7. 1–24
Ps. 99; 100; *111* *alt.* Ps. 94 Amos ch. 9 1 Cor. 7. 25–end **Wr** *or* **Gr**	**Prisca, Martyr at Rome, c. 265** For the Week of Prayer for Christian Unity, see *Common Worship* provision. Com. Virgin Martyr Gen. 8.15 – 9.7 Matt. 25. 1–13	Amos ch. 9 1 Cor. 7. 25–end
Ps. 73 *alt.* Ps. 102 Hos. 1.1 – 2.1 1 Cor. ch. 8 **W** *or* **G**		Gen. 9. 8–19 Matt. 25. 14–30	Hos. 1.1 – 2.1 1 Cor. ch. 8
Ps. *61*; 66 *alt.* Ps. 104 Hos. 2. 2–17 1 Cor. 9. 1–14 ct **Wr** *or* **Gr**	**Fabian, Bishop of Rome, Martyr, 250** Com. Martyr Gen. 11. 1–9 Matt. 25. 31–end	Hos. 2. 2–17 1 Cor. 9. 1–14 ct
Ps. 33 (*or* 33. 1–12) Jer. 3.21 – 4.2 Titus 2. 1–8, 11–14 *Gospel:* Matt. 4. 12–23 **W** *or* **G**	**THE THIRD SUNDAY AFTER THE EPIPHANY** 2 Kings 6. 14b–23 Ps. 102. 15–22 Rom. 12. 16b–end Matt. 8. 1–13	Ps. 113 Jonah 3. 1–5, 10 John 3. 16–21	Ps. 33 (*or* 33. 1–12) Jer. 3.21 – 4.2 Titus 2. 1–8, 11–14

January 2018

	Sunday Principal Service / Weekday Eucharist	Third Service / Morning Prayer

22 DEL 3

M Vincent of Saragossa, Deacon, first Martyr of Spain, 304
2 Sam. 5. 1–7, 10
Ps. 89. 19–27
Mark 3. 22–30

Ps. 40; *108*
alt. Ps. *98*; 99; 101
Gen. 11.27 – 12.9

W
Matt. 26. 1–16

23

Tu
2 Sam. 6. 12–15, 17–19
Ps. 24. 7–end
Mark 3. 31–end

Ps. 34; *36*
alt. Ps. 106† (or Ps. 103)
Gen. 13. 2–end

W
Matt. 26. 17–35

24

W **Francis de Sales, Bishop of Geneva, Teacher, 1622**
Com. Teacher   *or* 2 Sam. 7. 4–17
also Prov. 3. 13–18   Ps. 89. 19–27
John 3. 17–21   Mark 4. 1–20

Ps. 45; *46*
alt. Ps. 110; *111*; 112
Gen. ch. 14
Matt. 26. 36–46

W

25

Th THE CONVERSION OF PAUL
Jer. 1. 4–10
or Acts 9. 1–22
Ps. 67
Acts 9. 1–22
or Gal. 1. 11–16a

MP: Ps. 66; 147. 13–end
Ezek. 3. 22–end
Phil. 3. 1–14

W
Matt. 19. 27–end

26

F **Timothy and Titus, Companions of Paul**
Isa. 61. 1–3a   *or* 2 Sam. 11. 1–10, 13–17
Ps. 100   Ps. 51. 1–6, 9
2 Tim. 2. 1–8   Mark 4. 26–34
or Titus 1. 1–5

Ps. 61; *65*
alt. Ps. 139
Gen. ch. 16

W Luke 10. 1–9
Matt. 26. 57–end

27

Sa
2 Sam. 12. 1–7, 10–17
Ps. 51. 11–16
Mark 4. 35–end

Ps. 68
alt. Ps. 120; *121*; 122
Gen. 17. 1–22

W
Matt. 27. 1–10

28

S THE FOURTH SUNDAY OF EPIPHANY
or The Presentation of Christ in the Temple*
Deut. 18. 15–20
Ps. 111
Rev. 12. 1–5a
Mark 1. 21–28

Ps. 71. 1–6, 15–17
Jer. 1. 4–10
Mark 1. 40–end

W

---

29 DEL 4

M **
2 Sam. 15. 13–14, 30; 16. 5–13
Ps. 3
Mark 5. 1–20

***Ps. *57*; 96
alt. Ps. 123; 124; 125; *126*
Gen. 18. 1–15

W [G]
Matt. 27. 11–26

30

Tu **Charles, King and Martyr, 1649**
Com. Martyr   *or* 2 Sam. 18.9–10, 14, 24–25,
also Ecclus. 2. 12–17   30 – 19.3
1 Tim. 6. 12–16   Ps. 86. 1–6
                               Mark. 5. 21–end

***Ps. *93*; 97
alt. Ps. *132*; 133
Gen. 18. 16–end
Matt. 27. 27–44

Wr [Gr]

31

W John Bosco, Priest, Founder of the Salesian Teaching Order, 1888
2 Sam. 24. 2, 9–17
Ps. 32. 1–8
Mark 6. 1–6a

***Ps. *95*; 98
alt. Ps. 119. 153–end
Gen. 19. 1–3, 12–29

W [G]
Matt. 27. 45–56

---

*See provision for First EP on 1 February and throughout the day for The Presentation on 2 February.
**Ordinary Time begins today if The Presentation was observed on 28 January.
***If The Presentation was observed on 28 January, the alternative psalms are used.

Second Service Evening Prayer	Calendar and Holy Communion	Morning Prayer	Evening Prayer
Ps. *138*; 144 *alt.* Ps. 105† *(or* Ps. 103) Hos. 2.18 – 3.end I Cor. 9. 15–end	**Vincent of Saragossa, Deacon, first Martyr of Spain, 304** Com. Martyr **Wr** *or* **Gr**	Gen. 11.27 – 12.9 Matt. 26. 1–16	Hos. 2.18 – 3.end I Cor. 9. 15–end
Ps. 145 *alt.* Ps. 107† Hos. 4. 1–16 I Cor. 10. 1–13	**W** *or* **G**	Gen. 13. 2–end Matt. 26. 17–35	Hos. 4. 1–16 I Cor. 10. 1–13
Ps. 21; *29* *alt.* Ps. 119. 129–152 Hos. 5. 1–7 I Cor. 10.14 – 11.1 *or First EP of The Conversion* *of Paul* Ps. 149 Isa. 49. 1–13 Acts 22. 3–16 ct	**W** *or* **G**	Gen. ch. 14 Matt. 26. 36–46	Hos. 5. 1–7 I Cor. 10.14 – 11.1 *or First EP of The* *Conversion of Paul* (Ps. 149) Isa. 49. 1–13 Acts 22. 3–16 **W ct**
EP: Ps. 119. 41–56 Ecclus. 39. 1–10 *or* Isa. 56. 1–8 Col. 1.24 – 2.7	THE CONVERSION OF PAUL Josh. 5. 13–end Ps. 67 Acts 9. 1–22 Matt. 19. 27–end **W**	(Ps. 66; 147. 13–end) Ezek. 3. 22–end Phil. 3. 1–14	(Ps. 119. 41–56) Ecclus. 39. 1–10 *or* Isa. 56. 1–8 Col. 1.24 – 2.7
Ps. *67*; 77 *alt.* Ps. *130*; 131; 137 Hos. 6.7 – 7.2 I Cor. 11. 17–end	**W** *or* **G**	Gen. ch. 16 Matt. 26. 57–end	Hos. 6.7 – 7.2 I Cor. 11. 17–end
Ps. *72*; 76 *alt.* Ps. 118 Hos. ch. 8 I Cor. 12. 1–11 ct	**W** *or* **G**	Gen. 17. 1–22 Matt. 27. 1–10	Hos. ch. 8 I Cor. 12. 1–11 ct
Ps. 34 *(or* 34. 1–10) I Sam. 3. 1–20 I Cor. 14. 12–20 *Gospel:* Matt. 13. 10–17	SEPTUAGESIMA Gen. 1. 1–5 Ps. 9. 10–20 I Cor. 9. 24–end Matt. 20. 1–16 **W** *or* **G**	Ps. 71. 1–6, 15–17 Jer. 1. 4–10 Mark 1. 40–end	Ps. 34 *(or* 34. 1–10) I Sam. 3. 1–20 I Cor. 14. 12–20
***Ps. 2; *20* *alt.* Ps. *127*; 128; 129 Hos. ch. 9 I Cor. 12. 12–end	**W** *or* **G**	Gen. 18. 1–15 Matt. 27. 11–26	Hos. ch. 9 I Cor. 12. 12–end
***Ps. *19*; 21 *alt.* Ps. (134); *135* Hos. ch. 10 I Cor. ch. 13	**Charles, King and Martyr, 1649** Com. Martyr **Wr** *or* **Gr**	Gen. 18. 16–end Matt. 27. 27–44	Hos. ch. 10 I Cor. ch. 13
***Ps. *81*; 111 *alt.* Ps. 136 Hos. 11. 1–11 I Cor. 14. 1–19	**W** *or* **G**	Gen. 19. 1–3, 12–29 Matt. 27. 45–56	Hos. 11. 1–11 I Cor. 14. 1–19

February 2018

| | Sunday Principal Service
Weekday Eucharist | Third Service
Morning Prayer |

---

1 Th   *Brigid, Abbess of Kildare, c. 525*

	I Kings 2. 1–4, 10–12	*Ps. 99; *110*
	Canticle: I Chron. 29. 10–12	alt. Ps. *143*; 146
	or Ps. 145. 1–5	Gen. 21. 1–21
	Mark 6. 7–13	Matt. 27. 57–end

W [G]

2 F   **THE PRESENTATION OF CHRIST IN THE TEMPLE (CANDLEMAS)**

	Mal. 3. 1–5	*MP:* Ps. *48*; 146
	Ps. 24. [1–6] 7–end	Exod. 13. 1–16
	Heb. 2. 14–end	Rom. 12. 1–5
ѯ	Luke 2. 22–40	

or, if The Presentation is observed on 28 January:

	Ecclus. 47. 2–11	Ps. 142; *144*
	Ps. 18. 31–36, 50–end	Gen. 22. 1–19
G	Mark 6. 14–29	Matt. 28. 1–15

---

3 Sa   **Anskar, Archbishop of Hamburg, Missionary in Denmark and Sweden, 865**
Ordinary Time starts today (or on 29 January if The Presentation is observed on 28 January)

	Com. Missionary	*or*	I Kings 3. 4–13	Ps. 147
	esp. Isa. 52. 7–10		Ps. 119. 9–16	Gen. ch. 23
	also Rom. 10. 11–15		Mark 6. 30–34	Matt. 28. 16–end
Gw				

---

4 S   THE SECOND SUNDAY BEFORE LENT **(Proper 1)**

	Prov. 8. 1, 22–31	Ps. 29; 67
	Ps. 104. 26–end	Deut. 8. 1–10
	Col. 1. 15–20	Matt. 6. 25–end
G	John 1. 1–14	

---

5 M
DEL 5

	I Kings 8. 1–7, 9–13	Ps. *1*; 2; 3
	Ps. 132. 1–9	Gen. 29.31 – 30.24
G	Mark 6. 53–end	2 Tim. 4. 1–8

---

6 Tu   *The Martyrs of Japan, 1597*
(The Accession of Queen Elizabeth II may be observed on 6 February, and Collect, Readings and
Post-Communion for the sovereign used.)

	I Kings 8. 22–23, 27–30	Ps. *5*; 6; (8)
	Ps. 84. 1–10	Gen. 31. 1–24
G	Mark 7. 1–13	2 Tim. 4. 9–end

---

7 W

	I Kings 10. 1–10	Ps. 119. 1–32
	Ps. 37. 3–6, 30–32	Gen. 31.25 – 32.2
G	Mark 7. 14–23	Titus ch. 1

---

8 Th

	I Kings 11. 4–13	Ps. 14; *15*; 16
	Ps. 106. 3, 35–41	Gen. 32. 3–30
G	Mark 7. 24–30	Titus ch. 2

---

9 F

	I Kings 11. 29–32; 12. 19	Ps. 17; *19*
	Ps. 81. 8–14	Gen. 33. 1–17
G	Mark 7. 31–end	Titus ch. 3

---

10 Sa   *Scholastica, sister of Benedict, Abbess of Plombariola, c. 543*

	I Kings 12. 26–32; 13. 33–end	Ps. 20; 21; *23*
	Ps. 106. 6–7, 20–23	Gen. ch. 35
	Mark 8. 1–10	Philemon
G		

---

*If The Presentation was observed on 28 January, the alternative psalms are used.

Second Service Evening Prayer	Calendar and Holy Communion	Morning Prayer	Evening Prayer
First EP of The Presentation Ps. 118 1 Sam. 1. 19b–end Heb. 4. 11–end ℣ ct *or, if The Presentation* *is observed on 28 January:* Ps. *138*; 140; 141 Hos. 11.12 – 12.end 1 Cor. 14. 20–end	**W** or **G**	Gen. 21. 1–21 Matt. 27. 57–end	*First EP of The* *Presentation* Ps. 118 1 Sam. 1. 19b–end Heb. 4. 11–end ℣ ct
EP: Ps. 122; *132* Hag. 2. 1–9 John 2. 18–22	**THE PRESENTATION OF CHRIST IN THE TEMPLE** Mal. 3. 1–5 Ps. 48. 1–7 Gal. 4. 1–7 Luke 2. 22–40	Ps. 48; 146 Exod. 13. 1–16 Rom. 12. 1–5	Ps. 122; 132 Hag. 2. 1–9 John 2. 18–22
Ps. 145 Hos. 13. 1–14 1 Cor. 16. 1–9	℣		
Ps. *148*; 149; 150 Hos. ch. 14 1 Cor. 16. 10–end ct	**Blasius, Bishop of Sebastopol, Martyr, c. 316** Com. Martyr **Gr**	Gen. ch. 23 Matt. 28. 16–end	Hos. ch. 14 1 Cor. 16. 10–end ct
Ps. 65 Gen. 2. 4b–end Luke 8. 22–35	**SEXAGESIMA** Gen. 3. 9–19 Ps. 83. 1–2, 13–end 2 Cor. 11. 19–31 **G** Luke 8. 4–15	Ps. 29; 67 Deut. 8. 1–10 Matt. 6. 25–end	Ps. 65 Gen. 2. 4b–end Luke 8. 22–35
Ps. *4*; 7 2 Chron. 9. 1–12 John 19. 1–16	**Agatha, Martyr in Sicily, 251** Com. Virgin Martyr **Gr**	Gen. 29.31 – 30.24 2 Tim. 4. 1–8	2 Chron. 9. 1–12 John 19. 1–16
Ps. *9*; 10† 2 Chron. 10.1 – 11.4 John 19. 17–30	**The Accession of Queen Elizabeth II, 1952** For Accession Service: Ps. 20; 101; 121; Josh. 1. 1–9; Prov. 8. 1–16; Rom. 13. 1–10; Rev. 21.22 – 22.4 For The Accession: 1 Pet. 2. 11–17 **G** Matt. 22. 16–22	Gen. 31. 1–24 2 Tim. 4. 9–end	2 Chron. 10.1 – 11.4 John 19. 17–30
Ps. *11*; 12; 13 2 Chron. ch. 12 John 19. 31–end	**G**	Gen. 31.25 – 32.2 Titus ch. 1	2 Chron. ch. 12 John 19. 31–end
Ps. 18† 2 Chron. 13.1 – 14.1 John 20. 1–10	**G**	Gen. 32. 3–30 Titus ch. 2	2 Chron. 13.1 – 14.1 John 20. 1–10
Ps. 22 2 Chron. 14. 2–end John 20. 11–18	**G**	Gen. 33. 1–17 Titus ch. 3	2 Chron. 14. 2–end John 20. 11–18
Ps. *24*; 25 2 Chron. 15. 1–15 John 20. 19–end ct	**G**	Gen. ch. 35 Philemon	2 Chron. 15. 1–15 John 20. 19–end ct

February 2018

			Sunday Principal Service / Weekday Eucharist	Third Service / Morning Prayer

11   S   THE SUNDAY NEXT BEFORE LENT

	Sunday Principal Service / Weekday Eucharist	Third Service / Morning Prayer
	2 Kings 2. 1–12	Ps. 27; 150
	Ps. 50. 1–6	Exod. 24. 12–end
	2 Cor. 4. 3–6	2 Cor. 3. 12–end
G	Mark 9. 2–9	

12   M   DEL 6   G

	James 1. 1–11	Ps. 27; **30**
	Ps. 119. 65–72	Gen. 37. 1–11
	Mark 8. 11–13	Gal. ch. 1

13   Tu   G

	James 1. 12–18	Ps. 32; **36**
	Ps. 94. 12–18	Gen. 37. 12–end
	Mark 8. 14–21	Gal. 2. 1–10

14   W   ASH WEDNESDAY

	Joel 2. 1–2, 12–17	MP: Ps. 38
	or Isa. 58. 1–12	Dan. 9. 3–6, 17–19
	Ps. 51. 1–18	1 Tim. 6. 6–19
	2 Cor. 5.20b – 6.10	
	Matt. 6. 1–6, 16–21	
P	or John 8. 1–11	

15   Th   *Sigfrid, Bishop, Apostle of Sweden, 1045; Thomas Bray, Priest, Founder of the SPCK and the SPG, 1730*

	Deut. 30. 15–end	Ps. 77
	Ps. 1	*alt.* Ps. 37†
	Luke 9. 22–25	Gen. ch. 39
P		Gal. 2. 11–end

16   F

	Isa. 58. 1–9a	Ps. **3**; 7
	Ps. 51. 1–5, 17–18	*alt.* Ps. 31
	Matt. 9. 14–15	Gen. ch. 40
P		Gal. 3. 1–14

17   Sa   **Janani Luwum, Archbishop of Uganda, Martyr, 1977**

	Com. Martyr	*or* Isa. 58. 9b–end	Ps. 71
	also Ecclus. 4. 20–28	Ps. 86. 1–7	*alt.* Ps. 41; **42**; 43
	John 12. 24–32	Luke 5. 27–32	Gen. 41. 1–24
Pr			Gal. 3. 15–22

18   S   THE FIRST SUNDAY OF LENT

	Gen. 9. 8–17	Ps. 77
	Ps. 25. 1–9	Exod. 34. 1–10
	1 Pet. 3. 18–end	Rom. 10. 8b–13
	Mark 1. 9–15	
P		

19   M

	Lev. 19. 1–2, 11–18	Ps. 10; *11*
	Ps. 19. 7–end	*alt.* Ps. 44
	Matt. 25. 31–end	Gen. 41. 25–45
P		Gal. 3.23 – 4.7

20   Tu

	Isa. 55. 10–11	Ps. 44
	Ps. 34. 4–6, 21–22	*alt.* Ps. **48**; 52
	Matt. 6. 7–15	Gen. 41.46 – 42.5
P		Gal. 4. 8–20

21   W   Ember Day*

	Jonah ch. 3	Ps. **6**; 17
	Ps. 51. 1–5, 17–18	*alt.* Ps. 119. 57–80
	Luke 11. 29–32	Gen. 42. 6–17
P		Gal. 4.21 – 5.1

22   Th

	Esther 14. 1–5, 12–14	Ps. **42**; 43
	or Isa. 55. 6–9	*alt.* Ps. 56; **57**; (63†)
	Ps. 138	Gen. 42. 18–28
P	Matt. 7. 7–12	Gal. 5. 2–15

*For Ember Day provision, see p. 11.

Second Service Evening Prayer		Calendar and Holy Communion	Morning Prayer	Evening Prayer
		QUINQUAGESIMA		
Ps. 2; [99]		Gen. 9. 8–17	Ps. 27; 150	Ps. 2; [99]
1 Kings 19. 1–16		Ps. 77. 11–end	Exod. 24. 12–end	1 Kings 19. 1–16
2 Pet. 1. 16–end		1 Cor. ch. 13	2 Cor. 3. 12–end	2 Pet. 1. 16–end
Gospel: Mark 9. [2–8] 9–13	G	Luke 18. 31–43		
Ps. 26; *28*; 29			Gen. 37. 1–11	Jer. ch. 1
Jer. ch. 1			Gal. ch. 1	John 3. 1–21
John 3. 1–21	G			
Ps. 33			Gen. 37. 12–end	Jer. 2. 1–13
Jer. 2. 1–13			Gal. 2. 1–10	John 3. 22–end
John 3. 22–end	G			
		ASH WEDNESDAY		
EP: Ps. *51* or Ps. 102		Ash Wed. Collect until 31 March	Ps. 38	Ps. 51 or Ps. 102
(or 102. 1–18)		Commination	Dan. 9. 3–6, 17–19	(or 102. 1–18)
Isa. 1. 10–18		Joel 2. 12–17	1 Tim. 6. 6–19	Isa. 1. 10–18
Luke 15. 11–end		Ps. 57		Luke 15. 11–end
		James 4. 1–10		
	P	Matt. 6. 16–21		
Ps. 74		Exod. 24. 12–end	Gen. ch. 39	Jer. 2. 14–32
alt. Ps. 39; *40*		Matt. 8. 5–13	Gal. 2. 11–end	John 4. 1–26
Jer. 2. 14–32				
John 4. 1–26	P			
Ps. 31		1 Kings 19. 3b–8	Gen. ch. 40	Jer. 3. 6–22
alt. Ps. 35		Matt. 5.43 – 6.6	Gal. 3. 1–14	John 4. 27–42
Jer. 3. 6–22				
John 4. 27–42	P			
Ps. 73		Isa. 38. 1–6a	Gen. 41. 1–24	Jer. 4. 1–18
alt. Ps. 45; *46*		Mark 6. 45–end	Gal. 3. 15–22	John 4. 43–end
Jer. 4. 1–18				
John 4. 43–end				
ct	P			ct
		THE FIRST SUNDAY IN LENT		
Ps. 119. 17–32		Collect	Ps. 77	Ps. 119. 17–32
Gen. 2. 15–17; 3. 1–7		(1) Lent 1	Exod. 34. 1–10	Gen. 2. 15–17; 3. 1–7
Rom. 5. 12–19		(2) Ash Wednesday	Rom. 10. 8b–13	Rom. 5. 12–19
or Luke 13. 31–end		Ember until 24 February		or Luke 13. 31–end
		Gen. 3. 1–6		
		Ps. 91. 1–12		
		2 Cor. 6. 1–10		
	P	Matt. 4. 1–11		
Ps. 12; *13*; 14		Ezek. 34. 11–16a	Gen. 41. 25–45	Jer. 4. 19–end
alt. Ps. *47*; 49		Matt. 25. 31–end	Gal. 3.23 – 4.7	John 5. 1–18
Jer. 4. 19–end				
John 5. 1–18	P			
Ps. 46; *49*		Isa. 55. 6–11	Gen. 41.46 – 42.5	Jer. 5. 1–19
alt. Ps. 50		Matt. 21. 10–16	Gal. 4. 8–20	John 5. 19–29
Jer. 5. 1–19				
John 5. 19–29	P			
		Ember Day		
Ps. 9; *28*		Ember CEG *or*	Gen. 42. 6–17	Jer. 5. 20–end
alt. Ps. *59*; 60 (67)		Isa. 58. 1–9a	Gal. 4.21 – 5.1	John 5. 30–end
Jer. 5. 20–end		Matt. 12. 38–end		
John 5. 30–end	P			
Ps. 137; 138; *142*		Isa. 58. 9b–end	Gen. 42. 18–28	Jer. 6. 9–21
alt. Ps. 61; *62*; 64		John 8. 31–45	Gal. 5. 2–15	John 6. 1–15
Jer. 6. 9–21				
John 6. 1–15	P			

February 2018

			Sunday Principal Service Weekday Eucharist	Third Service Morning Prayer
23	F	**Polycarp, Bishop of Smyrna, Martyr, c. 155** Ember Day* Com. Martyr *or* *also* Rev. 2. 8–11	Ezek. 18. 21–28 Ps. 130 Matt. 5. 20–26	Ps. 22 *alt.* Ps. *51*; 54 Gen. 42. 29–end Gal. 5. 16–end
	Pr			
24	Sa	Ember Day**	Deut. 26. 16–end Ps. 119. 1–8 Matt. 5. 43–end	Ps. 59; *63* *alt.* Ps. 68 Gen. 43. 1–15 Gal. ch. 6
	P			
25	S	THE SECOND SUNDAY OF LENT	Gen. 17. 1–7, 15–16 Ps. 22. 23–end Rom. 4. 13–end Mark 8. 31–end	Ps. 105. 1–6, 37–end Isa. 51. 1–11 Gal. 3. 1–9, 23–end
	P			
26	M		Dan. 9. 4–10 Ps. 79. 8–9, 12, 14 Luke 6. 36–38	Ps. 26; *32* *alt.* Ps. 71 Gen. 43. 16–end Heb. ch. 1
	P			
27	T	**George Herbert, Priest, Poet, 1633** Com. Pastor *or* *esp.* Mal. 2. 5–7 Matt. 11. 25–30 *also* Rev. 19. 5–9	Isa. 1. 10, 16–20 Ps. 50. 8, 16–end Matt. 23. 1–12	Ps. 50 *alt.* Ps. 73 Gen. 44. 1–17 Heb. 2. 1–9
	Pw			
28	W		Jer. 18. 18–20 Ps. 31. 4–5, 14–18 Matt. 20. 17–28	Ps. 35 *alt.* Ps. 77 Gen. 44. 18–end Heb. 2. 10–end
	P			

March 2018

1	Th	**David, Bishop of Menevia, Patron of Wales, c. 601** Com. Bishop *or* *also* 2 Sam. 23. 1–4 Ps. 89. 19–22, 24	Jer. 17. 5–10 Ps. 1 Luke 16. 19–end	Ps. 34 *alt.* Ps. 78. 1–39† Gen. 45. 1–15 Heb. 3. 1–6
	Pw			
2	F	**Chad, Bishop of Lichfield, Missionary, 672*** Com. Missionary *or* *also* 1 Tim. 6. 11b–16	Gen. 37. 3–4, 12–13, 17–28 Ps. 105. 16–22 Matt. 21. 33–43, 45–46	Ps. 40; *41* *alt.* Ps. 55 Gen. 45. 16–end Heb. 3. 7–end
	Pw			
3	Sa		Mic. 7. 14–15, 18–20 Ps. 103. 1–4, 9–12 Luke 15. 1–3, 11–end	Ps. 3; *25* *alt.* Ps. *76*; 79 Gen. 46. 1–7, 28–end Heb. 4. 1–13
	P			
4	S	THE THIRD SUNDAY OF LENT	Exod. 20. 1–17 Ps. 19 (or 19. 7–end) 1 Cor. 1. 18–25 John 2. 13–22	Ps. 18. 1–25 Jer. ch. 38 Phil. 1. 1–26
	P			
5	M	****	2 Kings 5. 1–15 Ps. 42. 1–2; 43. 1–4 Luke 4. 24–30	Ps. *5*; 7 *alt.* Ps. *80*; 82 Gen. 47. 1–27 Heb. 4.14 – 5.10
	P			

*For Ember Day provision, see p. 11.   **Matthias may be celebrated on 24 February instead of 14 May.
***Chad may be celebrated with Cedd on 26 October instead of 2 March.
****The following readings may replace those provided for Holy Communion on any day during the Third Week of Lent: Exod. 17. 1–7;
Ps. 95. 1–2, 6–end; John 4. 5–42.

Second Service Evening Prayer		Calendar and Holy Communion	Morning Prayer	Evening Prayer
Ps. 54; **55** alt. Ps. 38 Jer. 6. 22–end John 6. 16–27	P	Ember Day Ember CEG or Ezek. 18. 20–25 John 5. 2–15	Gen. 42. 29–end Gal. 5. 16–end	Jer. 6. 22–end John 6. 16–27 or First EP of Matthias (Ps. 147) Isa. 22. 15–22 Phil. 3.13b – 4.1 **R** ct
Ps. **4**; 16 alt. Ps. 65; **66** Jer. 7. 1–20 John 6. 27–40 ct	R	MATTHIAS THE APOSTLE Ember Day I Sam. 2. 27–35 Ps. 16. 1–7 Acts 1. 15–end Matt. 1. 25–end	(Ps. 15) Jonah 1. 1–9 Acts 2. 37–end	(Ps. 80) I Sam. 16. 1–13a Matt. 7. 15–27
Ps. 135 (or 135. 1–14) Gen. 12. 1–9 Heb. 11. 1–3, 8–16 Gospel: John 8. 51–end	P	THE SECOND SUNDAY IN LENT Jer. 17. 5–10 Ps. 25. 13–end I Thess. 4. 1–8 Matt. 15. 21–28	Ps. 105. 1–6, 37–end Isa. 51. 1–11 Gal. 3. 1–9, 23–end	Ps. 135 (or 135. 1–14) Gen. 12. 1–9 Heb. 11. 1–3, 8–16
Ps. 70; **74** alt. Ps. **72**; 75 Jer. 7. 21–end John 6. 41–51	P	Heb. 2. 1–10 John 8. 21–30	Gen. 43. 16–end Heb. ch. 1	Jer. 7. 21–end John 6. 41–51
Ps. **52**; 53; 54 alt. Ps. 74 Jer. 8. 1–15 John 6. 52–59	P	Heb. 2. 11–end Matt. 23. 1–12	Gen. 44. 1–17 Heb. 2. 1–9	Jer. 8. 1–15 John 6. 52–59
Ps. **3**; 51 alt. Ps. 119. 81–104 Jer. 8.18 – 9.11 John 6. 60–end	P	Heb. 3. 1–6 Matt. 20. 17–28	Gen. 44. 18–end Heb. 2. 10–end	Jer. 8.18 – 9.11 John 6. 60–end
Ps. 71 alt. Ps. 78. 40–end† Jer. 9. 12–24 John 7. 1–13	Pw	David, Bishop of Menevia, Patron of Wales, c. 601 Com. Bishop or Heb. 3. 7–end John 5. 30–end	Gen. 45. 1–15 Heb. 3. 1–6	Jer. 9. 12–24 John 7. 1–13
Ps. **6**; 38 alt. Ps. 69 Jer. 10. 1–16 John 7. 14–24	Pw	Chad, Bishop of Lichfield, Missionary, 672 Com. Bishop or Heb. ch. 4 Matt. 21. 33–end	Gen. 45. 16–end Heb. 3. 7–end	Jer. 10. 1–16 John 7. 14–24
Ps. **23**; 27 alt. Ps. 81; **84** Jer. 10. 17–24 John 7. 25–36 ct	P	Heb. ch. 5 Luke 15. 11–end	Gen. 46. 1–7, 28–end Heb. 4. 1–13	Jer. 10. 17–24 John 7. 25–36 ct
Ps. 11; 12 Exod. 5.1 – 6.1 Phil. 3. 4b–14 or Matt. 10. 16–22	P	THE THIRD SUNDAY IN LENT Num. 22. 21–31 Ps. 9. 13–end Eph. 5. 1–14 Luke 11. 14–28	Ps. 18. 1–25 Jer. ch. 38 Phil. 1. 1–26	Ps. 11; 12 Exod. 5.1 – 6.1 Phil. 3. 4b–14 or Matt. 10. 16–22
Ps. 11; **17** alt. Ps. **85**; 86 Jer. 11. 1–17 John 7. 37–52	P	Heb. 6. 1–10 Luke 4. 23–30	Gen. 47. 1–27 Heb. 4.14 – 5.10	Jer. 11. 1–17 John 7. 37–52

March 2018

			Sunday Principal Service Weekday Eucharist	Third Service Morning Prayer
6	Tu P		Song of the Three 2, 11–20 or Dan. 2. 20–23 Ps. 25. 3–10 Matt. 18. 21–end	Ps. 6; **9** alt. Ps. 87; **89. 1–18** Gen. 47.28 – 48.end Heb. 5.11 – 6.12
7	W Pr	**Perpetua, Felicity and their Companions, Martyrs at Carthage, 203** Com. Martyr or esp. Rev. 12. 10–12a also Wisd. 3. 1–7	 Deut. 4. 1, 5–9 Ps. 147. 13–end Matt. 5. 17–19	Ps. 38 alt. Ps. 119. 105–128 Gen. 49. 1–32 Heb. 6. 13–end
8	Th Pw	**Edward King, Bishop of Lincoln, 1910** Felix, Bishop, Apostle to the East Angles, 647; Geoffrey Studdert Kennedy, Priest, Poet, 1929 Com. Bishop or also Heb. 13. 1–8	 Jer. 7. 23–28 Ps. 95. 1–2, 6–end Luke 11. 14–23	Ps. **56**; 57 alt. Ps. 90; **92** Gen. 49.33 – 50.end Heb. 7. 1–10
9	F P		Hos. ch. 14 Ps. 81. 6–10, 13, 16 Mark 12. 28–34	Ps. 22 alt. Ps. **88**; (95) Exod. 1. 1–14 Heb. 7. 11–end
10	Sa P		Hos. 5.15 – 6.6 Ps. 51. 1–2, 17–end Luke 18. 9–14	Ps. 31 alt. Ps. 96; **97**; 100 Exod. 1.22 – 2.10 Heb. ch. 8
11	S P	THE FOURTH SUNDAY OF LENT (Mothering Sunday) or, for Mothering Sunday:	Num. 21. 4–9 Ps. 107. 1–3, 17–22 (or 107. 1–9) Eph. 2. 1–10 John 3. 14–21 Exod. 2. 1–10 or 1 Sam. 1. 20–end Ps. 34. 11–20 or Ps. 127. 1–4 2 Cor. 1. 3–7 or Col. 3. 12–17 Luke 2. 33–35 or John 19. 25b–27	Ps. 27 1 Sam. 16. 1–13 John 9. 1–25
12	M * P		Isa. 65. 17–21 Ps. 30. 1–5, 8, 11–end John 4. 43–end	Ps. 70; **77** alt. Ps. **98**; 99; 101 Exod. 2. 11–22 Heb. 9. 1–14
13	Tu P		Ezek. 47. 1–9, 12 Ps. 46. 1–8 John 5. 1–3, 5–16	Ps. 54; **79** alt. Ps. **106†** (or 103) Exod. 2.23 – 3.20 Heb. 9. 15–end
14	W P		Isa. 49. 8–15 Ps. 145. 8–18 John 5. 17–30	Ps. **63**; 90 alt. Ps. 110; **111**; 112 Exod. 4. 1–23 Heb. 10. 1–18
15	Th P		Exod. 32. 7–14 Ps. 106. 19–23 John 5. 31–end	Ps. 53; **86** alt. Ps. 113; **115** Exod. 4.27 – 6.1 Heb. 10. 19–25

*The following readings may replace those provided for Holy Communion on any day during the Fourth Week of Lent: Mic. 7. 7–9; Ps. 27. 1, 9–10, 16–17; John ch. 9.

Second Service Evening Prayer		Calendar and Holy Communion	Morning Prayer	Evening Prayer
Ps. 61; 62; **64** alt. Ps. 89. 19–end Jer. 11.18 – 12.6 John 7.53 – 8.11	P	Heb. 6. 11–end Matt. 18. 15–22	Gen. 47.28 – 48.end Heb. 5.11 – 6.12	Jer. 11.18 – 12.6 John 7.53 – 8.11
Ps. 36; **39** alt. Ps. **91**; 93 Jer. 13. 1–11 John 8. 12–30	Pr	**Perpetua, Martyr at Carthage, 203** Com. Martyr or Heb. 7. 1–10 Matt. 15. 1–20	Gen. 49. 1–32 Heb. 6. 13–end	Jer. 13. 1–11 John 8. 12–30
Ps. **59**; 60 alt. Ps. 94 Jer. ch. 14 John 8. 31–47	P	Heb. 7. 11–25 John 6. 26–35	Gen. 49.33 – 50.end Heb. 7. 1–10	Jer. ch. 14 John 8. 31–47
Ps. 69 alt. Ps. 102 Jer. 15. 10–end John 8. 48–end	P	Heb. 7. 26–end John 4. 5–26	Exod. 1. 1–14 Heb. 7. 11–end	Jer. 15. 10–end John 8. 48–end
Ps. **116**; 130 alt. Ps. 104 Jer. 16.10 – 17.4 John 9. 1–17 ct	P	Heb. 8. 1–6 John 8. 1–11	Exod. 1.22 – 2.10 Heb. ch. 8	Jer. 16.10 – 17.4 John 9. 1–17 ct
Ps. 13; 14 Exod. 6. 2–13 Rom. 5. 1–11 *Gospel:* John 12. 1–8 *If the Principal Service readings for The Fourth Sunday of Lent are displaced by Mothering Sunday provisions, they may be used at the Second Service.*	P	**THE FOURTH SUNDAY IN LENT** To celebrate Mothering Sunday, see *Common Worship* provision. Exod. 16. 2–7a Ps. 122 Gal. 4. 21–end or Heb. 12. 22–24 John 6. 1–14	Ps. 27 1 Sam. 16. 1–13 John 9. 1–25	Ps. 13; 14 Exod. 6. 2–13 Rom. 5. 1–11
Ps. **25**; 28 alt. Ps. **105**† (or 103) Jer. 17. 5–18 John 9. 18–end	Pw	**Gregory the Great, Bishop of Rome, 604** Com. Doctor or Heb. 11. 1–6 John 2. 13–end	Exod. 2. 11–22 Heb. 9. 1–14	Jer. 17. 5–18 John 9. 18–end
Ps. **80**; 82 alt. Ps. 107† Jer. 18. 1–12 John 10. 1–10	P	Heb. 11. 13–16a John 7. 14–24	Exod. 2.23 – 3.20 Heb. 9. 15–end	Jer. 18. 1–12 John 10. 1–10
Ps. 52; **91** alt. Ps. 119. 129–152 Jer. 18. 13–end John 10. 11–21	P	Heb. 12. 1–11 John 9. 1–17	Exod. 4. 1–23 Heb. 10. 1–18	Jer. 18. 13–end John 10. 11–21
Ps. 94 alt. Ps. 114; **116**; 117 Jer. 19. 1–13 John 10. 22–end	P	Heb. 12. 12–17 John 5. 17–27	Exod. 4.27 – 6.1 Heb. 10. 19–25	Jer. 19. 1–13 John 10. 22–end

March 2018

		Sunday Principal Service / Weekday Eucharist	Third Service / Morning Prayer

March 2018 — Sunday Principal Service / Weekday Eucharist · Third Service / Morning Prayer

16
F

Wisd. 2. 1, 12–22
or Jer. 26. 8–11
Ps. 34. 15–end
John 7. 1–2, 10, 25–30

Ps. 102
alt. Ps. 139
Exod. 6. 2–13
Heb. 10. 26–end

P

17
Sa

Patrick, Bishop, Missionary, Patron of Ireland, c. 460
Com. Missionary   or   Jer. 11. 18–20
also Ps. 91. 1–4, 13–end   Ps. 7. 1–2, 8–10
Luke 10. 1–12, 17–20   John 7. 40–52

Ps. 32
alt. Ps. 120; *121*; 122
Exod. 7. 8–end
Heb. 11. 1–16

Pw

18
S

THE FIFTH SUNDAY IN LENT (Passiontide begins)
Jer. 31. 31–34
Ps. 51. 1–13
or Ps. 119. 9–16
Heb. 5. 5–10
John 12. 20–33

Ps. 107. 1–22
Exod. 24. 3–8
Heb. 12. 18–end

P

19
M*

JOSEPH OF NAZARETH
2 Sam. 7. 4–16
Ps. 89. 26–36
Rom. 4. 13–18
Matt. 1. 18–end

MP: Ps. 25; 147. 1–12
Isa. 11. 1–10
Matt. 13. 54–end

W

20
Tu

Cuthbert, Bishop of Lindisfarne, Missionary, 687**
Com. Missionary   or   Num. 21. 4–9
esp. Ezek. 34. 11–16   Ps. 102. 1–3, 16–23
also Matt. 18. 12–14   John 8. 21–30

Ps. *35*; 123
alt. Ps. *132*; 133
Exod. 8. 20–end
Heb. 11.32 – 12.2

Pw

21
W

Thomas Cranmer, Archbishop of Canterbury, Reformation Martyr, 1556
Com. Martyr   or   Dan. 3. 14–20, 24–25, 28
Canticle: Bless the Lord
John 8. 31–42

Ps. *55*; 124
alt. Ps. 119. 153–end
Exod. 9. 1–12
Heb. 12. 3–13

Pr

22
Th

Gen. 17. 3–9
Ps. 105. 4–9
John 8. 51–end

Ps. *40*; 125
alt. Ps. *143*; 146
Exod. 9. 13–end
Heb. 12. 14–end

P

23
F

Jer. 20. 10–13
Ps. 18. 1–6
John 10. 31–end

Ps. *22*; 126
alt. Ps. 142; *144*
Exod. ch. 10
Heb. 13. 1–16

P

24
Sa

Walter Hilton of Thurgarton, Augustinian Canon, Mystic, 1396; Paul Couturier, Priest, Ecumenist, 1953; Oscar Romero, Archbishop of San Salvador, Martyr, 1980
Ezek. 37. 21–end
Canticle: Jer. 31. 10–13
or Ps. 121
John 11. 45–end

Ps. *23*; 127
alt. Ps. 147
Exod. ch. 11
Heb. 13. 17–end

P

25
S

PALM SUNDAY
(The Annunciation transferred to 9 April)
Liturgy of the Palms   Liturgy of the Passion
Mark 11. 1–11   Isa. 50. 4–9a
or John 12. 12–16   Ps. 31. 9–16 (or 31. 9–18)
Ps. 118. 1–2, 19–end   Phil. 2. 5–11
(or 118. 19–end)   Mark 14.1 – 15.end
          or Mark 15. 1–39 [40–end]

Ps. 61; 62
Zech. 9. 9–12
1 Cor. 2. 1–12

R

---

*The following readings may replace those provided for Holy Communion on any day, except St Joseph's Day, during the Fifth Week of Lent: 2 Kings 4. 18–21, 32–37; Ps. 17. 1–8, 16; John 11. 1–45.

**Cuthbert may be celebrated on 4 September instead of 20 March.

Second Service Evening Prayer	Calendar and Holy Communion		Morning Prayer	Evening Prayer
Ps. 13; *16* alt. Ps. *130*; 131; 137 Jer. 19.14 – 20.6 John 11. 1–16	Heb. 12. 22–end John 11. 33–46	P	Exod. 6. 2–13 Heb. 10. 26–end	Jer. 19.14 – 20.6 John 11. 1–16
Ps. *140*; 141; 142 alt. Ps. 118 Jer. 20. 7–end John 11. 17–27 ct	Heb. 13. 17–21 John 8. 12–20	P	Exod. 7. 8–end Heb. 11. 1–16	Jer. 20. 7–end John 11. 17–27 ct
Ps. 34 (or 34. 1–10) Exod. 7. 8–24 Rom. 5. 12–end *Gospel:* Luke 22. 1–13 or First EP of Joseph Ps. 132 Hos. 11. 1–9 Luke 2. 41–end **W** ct	**THE FIFTH SUNDAY IN LENT** Exod. 24. 4–8 Ps. 143 Heb. 9. 11–15 John 8. 46–end	P	Ps. 107. 1–22 Jer. 31. 31–34 Heb. 5. 5–10	Ps. 34 (or 34. 1–10) Exod. 7. 8–24 Rom. 5. 12–end
EP: Ps. 1; 112 Gen. 50. 22–end Matt. 2. 13–end	To celebrate Joseph, see *Common Worship* provision. Col. 1. 13–23a John 7. 1–13	P	Exod. 8. 1–19 Heb. 11. 17–31	Jer. 21. 1–10 John 11. 28–44
Ps. *61*; 64 alt. Ps. (134); *135* Jer. 22. 1–5, 13–19 John 11. 45–end	Col. 2. 8–12 John 7. 32–39	P	Exod. 8. 20–end Heb. 11.32 – 12.2	Jer. 22. 1–5, 13–19 John 11. 45–end
Ps. 56; *62* alt. Ps. 136 Jer. 22.20 – 23.8 John 12. 1–11	**Benedict, Abbot of Monte Cassino, c. 550** Com. Abbot or Col. 2. 13–19 John 7. 40–end	Pw	Exod. 9. 1–12 Heb. 12. 3–13	Jer. 22.20 – 23.8 John 12. 1–11
Ps. 42; *43* alt. Ps. *138*; 140; 141 Jer. 23. 9–32 John 12. 12–19	Col. 3. 8–11 John 10. 22–38	P	Exod. 9. 13–end Heb. 12. 14–end	Jer. 23. 9–32 John 12. 12–19
Ps. 31 alt. Ps. 145 Jer. ch. 24 John 12. 20–36a	Col. 3. 12–17 John 11. 47–54	P	Exod. ch. 10 Heb. 13. 1–16	Jer. ch. 24 John 12. 20–36a
Ps. 128; 129; *130* alt. Ps. *148*; 149; 150 Jer. 25. 1–14 John 12. 36b–end ct	Col. 4. 2–6 John 6. 53–end	P	Exod. ch. 11 Heb. 13. 17–end	Jer. 25. 1–14 John 12. 36b–end ct
Ps. 69. 1–20 Isa. 5. 1–7 Mark 12. 1–12	**THE SUNDAY NEXT BEFORE EASTER (PALM SUNDAY)** (*The Annunciation transferred to 9 April*) Zech. 9. 9–12 Ps. 73. 22–end Phil. 2. 5–11 Passion acc. to Matthew Matt. 27. 1–54 or Matt. 26.1 – 27.61 or Matt. 21. 1–13	R	Ps. 61; 62 Isa. 42. 1–9 1 Cor. 2. 1–12	Ps. 69. 1–20 Isa. 5. 1–7 Mark 12. 1–12

March 2018

			Sunday Principal Service Weekday Eucharist	Third Service Morning Prayer
26	M	MONDAY OF HOLY WEEK	Isa. 42. 1–9 Ps. 36. 5–11 Heb. 9. 11–15	MP: Ps. 41 Lam. 1. 1–12a Luke 22. 1–23
	R		John 12. 1–11	
27	Tu	TUESDAY OF HOLY WEEK	Isa. 49. 1–7 Ps. 71. 1–14 (or 71. 1–8) 1 Cor. 1. 18–31	MP: Ps. 27 Lam. 3. 1–18 Luke 22. [24–38] 39–53
	R		John 12. 20–36	
28	W	WEDNESDAY OF HOLY WEEK	Isa. 50. 4–9a Ps. 70 Heb. 12. 1–3	MP: Ps. 102 (or 102. 1–18) Wisd. 1.16 – 2.1, 12–22 or Jer. 11. 18–20
	R		John 13. 21–32	Luke 22. 54–end
29	Th	**MAUNDY THURSDAY**	Exod. 12. 1–14 (or 12. 1–4, 11–14) Ps. 116. 1, 10–end (or 116. 9–end) 1 Cor. 11. 23–26	MP: Ps. 42; 43 Lev. 16. 2–24 Luke 23. 1–25
	W(HC)R		John 13. 1–17, 31b–35	
30	F	**GOOD FRIDAY**	Isa. 52.13 – 53.end Ps. 22 (or 22. 1–11 or 22. 1–21) Heb. 10. 16–25 or Heb. 4. 14–16; 5. 7–9 John 18.1 – 19.end	MP: Ps. 69 Gen. 22. 1–18 A part of John 18 – 19 if not read at the Principal Service or Heb. 10. 1–10
	R			
31	Sa	EASTER EVE These readings are for use at services other than the Easter Vigil.	Job 14. 1–14 or Lam. 3. 1–9, 19–24 Ps. 31. 1–4, 15–16 (or 31. 1–5) 1 Pet. 4. 1–8 Matt. 27. 57–end or John 19. 38–end	Ps. 142 Hos. 6. 1–6 John 2. 18–22

April 2018

1	S	**EASTER DAY** The following readings and psalms (or canticles) are provided for use at the Easter Vigil. A minimum of three Old Testament readings should be chosen. The reading from Exodus ch. 14 should always be used.	Gen. 1.1 – 2.4a & Ps. 136. 1–9, 23–end Gen. 7. 1–5, 11–18; 8. 6–18; 9. 8–13 & Ps. 46 Gen. 22. 1–18 & Ps. 16 Exod. 14. 10–end; 15. 20–21 & Canticle: Exod. 15. 1b–13, 17–18 Isa. 55. 1–11 & Canticle: Isa. 12. 2–end Baruch 3.9–15, 32 – 4.4 & Ps. 19 or Prov. 8. 1–8, 19–21; 9. 4b–6 & Ps. 19 Ezek. 36. 24–28 & Ps. 42; 43 Ezek. 37. 1–14 & Ps. 143 Zeph. 3. 14–end & Ps. 98 Rom. 6. 3–11 & Ps. 114	
	𝍩		Mark 16. 1–8	
		Easter Day Services The reading from Acts must be used as either the first or second reading at the Principal Service.	Acts 10. 34–43 or Isa. 25. 6–9 Ps. 118. 1–2, 14–24 (or 118. 14–24) 1 Cor. 15. 1–11 or Acts 10. 34–43 John 20. 1–18	MP: Ps. 114; 117 Gen. 1. 1–5, 26–end 2 Cor. 5.14 – 6.2
	𝍩		or Mark 16. 1–8	

Second Service Evening Prayer		Calendar and Holy Communion	Morning Prayer	Evening Prayer
EP: Ps. 25 Lam. 2. 8–19 Col. 1. 18–23		**MONDAY IN HOLY WEEK** Isa. 63. 1–19 Ps. 55. 1–8 Gal. 6. 1–11 **R** Mark ch. 14	Ps. 41 Lam. 1. 1–12a John 12. 1–11	Ps. 25 Lam. 2. 8–19 Col. 1. 18–23
EP: Ps. 55. 13–24 Lam. 3. 40–51 Gal. 6. 11–end		**TUESDAY IN HOLY WEEK** Isa. 50. 5–11 Ps. 13 Rom. 5. 6–19 **R** Mark 15. 1–39	Ps. 27 Lam. 3. 1–18 John 12. 20–36	Ps. 55. 13–24 Lam. 3. 40–51 Gal. 6. 11–end
EP: Ps. 88 Isa. 63. 1–9 Rev. 14.18 – 15.4		**WEDNESDAY IN HOLY WEEK** Isa. 49. 1–9a Ps. 54 Heb. 9. 16–end **R** Luke ch. 22	Ps. 102 (or 102. 1–18) Wisd. 1.16 – 2.1, 12–22 or Jer. 11. 18–20 John 13. 21–32	Ps. 88 Isa. 63. 1–9 Rev. 14.18 – 15.4
EP: Ps. 39 Exod. ch. 11 Eph. 2. 11–18		**MAUNDY THURSDAY** Exod. 12. 1–11 Ps. 43 1 Cor. 11. 17–end Luke 23. 1–49 W(HC)R	Ps. 42; 43 Lev. 16. 2–24 John 13. 1–17, 31b–35	Ps. 39 Exod. ch. 11 Eph. 2. 11–18
EP: Ps. 130; 143 Lam. 5. 15–end *A part of* John 18 – 19 *if not read at the Principal Service, esp.* John 19. 38–end *or* Col. 1. 18–23		**GOOD FRIDAY** Alt. Collect Passion acc. to John Alt. Gospel, if Passion is read Num. 21. 4–9 Ps. 140. 1–9 Heb. 10. 1–25 John 19. 1–37 **R** or John 19. 38–end	Ps. 69 Gen. 22. 1–18 John ch. 18	Ps. 130; 143 Lam. 5. 15–end John 19. 38–end
Ps. 116 Job 19. 21–27 1 John 5. 5–12		**EASTER EVE** Job 14. 1–14 1 Pet. 3. 17–22 Matt. 27. 57–end	Ps. 142 Hos. 6. 1–6 John 2. 18–22	Ps. 116 Job 19. 21–27 1 John 5. 5–12
		EASTER DAY Exod. 12. 21–28 Ps. 111 Col. 3. 1–7 John 20. 1–10	Ps. 114; 117 Gen. 1. 1–5, 26–end 2 Cor. 5.14 – 6.2	Ps. 105 or Ps. 66. 1–11 Isa. 25. 6–9 Luke 24. 13–35
EP: Ps. 105 or Ps. 66. 1–11 Ezek. 37. 1–14 Luke 24. 13–35		♏		

April 2018

			Sunday Principal Service Weekday Eucharist	Third Service Morning Prayer
2	M W	MONDAY OF EASTER WEEK	Acts 2. 14, 22–32 Ps. 16. 1–2, 6–end Matt. 28. 8–15	Ps. *111*; 117; 146 Exod. 12. 1–14 1 Cor. 15. 1–11
3	Tu W	TUESDAY OF EASTER WEEK	Acts 2. 36–41 Ps. 33. 4–5, 18–end John 20. 11–18	Ps. *112*; 147. 1–12 Exod. 12. 14–36 1 Cor. 15. 12–19
4	W R	WEDNESDAY OF EASTER WEEK	Acts 3. 1–10 Ps. 105. 1–9 Luke 24. 13–35	Ps. *113*; 147. 13–end Exod. 12. 37–end 1 Cor. 15. 20–28
5	Th W	THURSDAY OF EASTER WEEK	Acts 3. 11–end Ps. 8 Luke 24. 35–48	Ps. *114*; 148 Exod. 13. 1–16 1 Cor. 15. 29–34
6	F W	FRIDAY OF EASTER WEEK	Acts 4. 1–12 Ps. 118. 1–4, 22–26 John 21. 1–14	Ps. *115*; 149 Exod. 13.17 – 14.14 1 Cor. 15. 35–50
7	Sa W	SATURDAY OF EASTER WEEK	Acts 4. 13–21 Ps. 118. 1–4, 14–21 Mark 16. 9–15	Ps. *116*; 150 Exod. 14. 15–end 1 Cor. 15. 51–end
8	S W	THE SECOND SUNDAY OF EASTER *The reading from Acts must be used as either the first or second reading at the Principal Service.*	Acts 4. 32–35 [or Exod. 14. 10–end; 15. 20–21] Ps. 133 1 John 1.1 – 2.2 John 20. 19–end	Ps. 22. 20–31 Isa. 53. 6–12 Rom. 4. 13–25
9	M Ⱳ	**THE ANNUNCIATION OF OUR LORD TO THE BLESSED VIRGIN MARY** (transferred from 25 March)	Isa. 7. 10–14 Ps. 40. 5–11 Heb. 10. 4–10 Luke 1. 26–38	*MP*: Ps. 111; 113 1 Sam. 2. 1–10 Rom. 5. 12–end
10	Tu W	**William Law, Priest, Spiritual Writer, 1761** *William of Ockham, Friar, Philosopher, Teacher, 1347* Com. Teacher or esp. 1 Cor. 2. 9–end *also* Matt. 17. 1–9	Acts 4. 32–end Ps. 93 John 3. 7–15	Ps. *8*; 20; 21 *alt.* Ps. *5*; 6; (8) Exod. 15.22 – 16.10 Col. 1. 15–end
11	W W	*George Augustus Selwyn, first Bishop of New Zealand, 1878*	Acts 5. 17–26 Ps. 34. 1–8 John 3. 16–21	Ps. 16; *30* *alt.* Ps. 119. 1–32 Exod. 16. 11–end Col. 2. 1–15
12	Th W		Acts 5. 27–33 Ps. 34. 1, 15–end John 3. 31–end	Ps. *28*; 29 *alt.* Ps. 14; *15*; 16 Exod. ch. 17 Col. 2.16 – 3.11

Second Service Evening Prayer	Calendar and Holy Communion	Morning Prayer	Evening Prayer
Ps. 135 Song of Sol. 1.9 – 2.7 Mark 16. 1–8	**MONDAY IN EASTER WEEK** Hos. 6. 1–6 Easter Anthems Acts 10. 34–43 W Luke 24. 13–35	Exod. 12. 1–14 I Cor. 15. 1–11	Song of Sol. 1.9 – 2.7 Mark 16. 1–8
Ps. 136 Song of Sol. 2. 8–end Luke 24. 1–12	**TUESDAY IN EASTER WEEK** I Kings 17. 17–end Ps. 16. 9–end Acts 13. 26–41 W Luke 24. 36b–48	Exod. 12. 14–36 I Cor. 15. 12–19	Song of Sol. 2. 8–end Luke 24. 1–12
Ps. 105 Song of Sol. ch. 3 Matt. 28. 16–end	Isa. 42. 10–16 Ps. 111 Acts 3. 12–18 W John 20. 11–18	Exod. 12. 37–end I Cor. 15. 20–28	Song of Sol. ch. 3 Matt. 28. 16–end
Ps. 106 Song of Sol. 5.2 – 6.3 Luke 7. 11–17	Isa. 43. 16–21 Ps. 113 Acts 8. 26–end W John 21. 1–14	Exod. 13. 1–16 I Cor. 15. 29–34	Song of Sol. 5.2 – 6.3 Luke 7. 11–17
Ps. 107 Song of Sol. 7.10 – 8.4 Luke 8. 41–end	Ezek. 37. 1–14 Ps. 116. 1–9 I Pet. 3. 18–end W Matt. 28. 16–end	Exod. 13.17 – 14.14 I Cor. 15. 35–50	Song of Sol. 7.10 – 8.4 Luke 8. 41–end
Ps. 145 Song of Sol. 8. 5–7 John 11. 17–44 ct	Zech. 8. 1–8 Ps. 118. 14–21 I Pet. 2. 1–10 W John 20. 24–end	Exod. 14. 15–end I Cor. 15. 51–end	Song of Sol. 8. 5–7 John 11. 17–44 ct
First EP of The Annunciation Ps. 85 Wisd. 9. 1–12 or Gen. 3. 8–15 Gal. 4. 1–5 ℣ ct	**THE FIRST SUNDAY AFTER EASTER** Ezek. 37. 1–10 Ps. 81. 1–4 I John 5. 4–12 John 20. 19–23 W	Ps. 22. 20–31 Isa. 53. 6–12 Rom. 4. 13–25	First EP of The Annunciation Ps. 85 Wisd. 9. 1–12 or Gen. 3. 8–15 Gal. 4. 1–5 ℣ ct
EP: Ps. 131; 146 Isa. 52. 1–12 Heb. 2. 5–end	**THE ANNUNCIATION OF THE BLESSED VIRGIN MARY** (transferred from 25 March) Isa. 7. 10–14 [15] Ps. 113 Rom. 5. 12–19 ℣ Luke 1. 26–38	Ps. 111 I Sam. 2. 1–10 Heb. 10. 4–10	Ps. 131; 146 Isa. 52. 1–12 Heb. 2. 5–end
Ps. 104 alt. Ps. 9; **10**† Deut. 1. 19–40 John 20. 11–18	W	Exod. 15.22 – 16.10 Col. 1. 15–end	Deut. 1. 19–40 John 20. 11–18
Ps. 33 alt. Ps. **11**; 12; 13 Deut. 3. 18–end John 20. 19–end	W	Exod. 16. 11–end Col. 2. 1–15	Deut. 3. 18–end John 20. 19–end
Ps. 34 alt. Ps. 18† Deut. 4. 1–14 John 21. 1–14	W	Exod. ch. 17 Col. 2.16 – 3.11	Deut. 4. 1–14 John 21. 1–14

April 2018

			Sunday Principal Service Weekday Eucharist	Third Service Morning Prayer
13	F		Acts 5. 34–42 Ps. 27. 1–5, 16–17 John 6. 1–15	Ps. 57; *61* *alt.* Ps. 17; *19* Exod. 18. 1–12
	W			Col. 3.12 – 4.1
14	Sa		Acts 6. 1–7 Ps. 33. 1–5, 18–19 John 6. 16–21	Ps. 63; *84* *alt.* Ps. 20; 21; *23* Exod. 18. 13–end
	W			Col. 4. 2–end
15	S	THE THIRD SUNDAY OF EASTER *The reading from Acts must be used as either the first or second reading at the Principal Service.*	Acts 3. 12–19 [or Zeph. 3. 14–end] Ps. 4 1 John 3. 1–7	Ps. 77. 11–20 Isa. 63. 7–15 1 Cor. 10. 1–13
	W		Luke 24. 36b–48	
16	M	*Isabella Gilmore, Deaconess, 1923*	Acts 6. 8–15 Ps. 119. 17–24 John 6. 22–29	Ps. *96*; 97 *alt.* Ps. 27; *30* Exod. ch. 19
	W			Luke 1. 1–25
17	Tu		Acts 7.51 – 8.1a Ps. 31. 1–5, 16 John 6. 30–35	Ps. *98*; 99; 100 *alt.* Ps. 32; *36* Exod. 20. 1–21
	W			Luke 1. 26–38
18	W		Acts 8. 1b–8 Ps. 66. 1–6 John 6. 35–40	Ps. 105 *alt.* Ps. 34 Exod. ch. 24
	W			Luke 1. 39–56
19	Th	**Alphege, Archbishop of Canterbury, Martyr, 1012** Com. Martyr *or* *also* Heb. 5. 1–4	Acts 8. 26–end Ps. 66. 7–8, 14–end John 6. 44–51	Ps. 136 *alt.* Ps. 37† Exod. 25. 1–22
	Wr			Luke 1. 57–end
20	F		Acts 9. 1–20 Ps. 117 John 6. 52–59	Ps. 107 *alt.* Ps. 31 Exod. 28. 1–4a, 29–38
	W			Luke 2. 1–20
21	Sa	**Anselm, Abbot of Le Bec, Archbishop of Canterbury, Teacher, 1109** Com. Teacher *or* *also* Wisd. 9. 13–end Rom. 5. 8–11	Acts 9. 31–42 Ps. 116. 10–15 John 6. 60–69	Ps. 108; *110*; 111 *alt.* Ps. 41; *42*; 43 Exod. 29. 1–9
	W			Luke 2. 21–40
22	S	THE FOURTH SUNDAY OF EASTER *The reading from Acts must be used as either the first or second reading at the Principal Service.*	Acts 4. 5–12 [Gen. 7. 1–5, 11–18; 8. 6–18; 9. 8–13] Ps. 23 1 John 3. 16–end John 10. 11–18	Ps. 119. 89–96 Neh. 7.73b – 8.12 Luke 24. 25–32
	W			
23	M	GEORGE, MARTYR, PATRON OF ENGLAND, c. 304	1 Macc. 2. 59–64 *or* Rev. 12. 7–12 Ps. 126 2 Tim. 2. 3–13	MP: Ps. 5; 146 Josh. 1. 1–9 Eph. 6. 10–20
	R		John 15. 18–21	

Second Service Evening Prayer		Calendar and Holy Communion	Morning Prayer	Evening Prayer
Ps. 118 alt. Ps. 22 Deut. 4. 15–31 John 21. 15–19	W		Exod. 18. 1–12 Col. 3.12 – 4.1	Deut. 4. 15–31 John 21. 15–19
Ps. 66 alt. Ps. 24; 25 Deut. 4. 32–40 John 21. 20–end ct	W		Exod. 18. 13–end Col. 4. 2–end	Deut. 4. 32–40 John 21. 20–end ct
Ps. 142 Deut. 7. 7–13 Rev. 2. 1–11 Gospel: Luke 16. 19–end	W	THE SECOND SUNDAY AFTER EASTER Ezek. 34. 11–16a Ps. 23 1 Pet. 2. 19–end John 10. 11–16	Ps. 77. 11–20 Isa. 63. 7–15 1 Cor. 10. 1–13	Ps. 142 Deut. 7. 7–13 Rev. 2. 1–11
Ps. 61; 65 alt. Ps. 26; 28; 29 Deut. 5. 1–22 Eph. 1. 1–14	W		Exod. ch. 19 Luke 1. 1–25	Deut. 5. 1–22 Eph. 1. 1–14
Ps. 71 alt. Ps. 33 Deut. 5. 22–end Eph. 1. 15–end	W		Exod. 20. 1–21 Luke 1. 26–38	Deut. 5. 22–end Eph. 1. 15–end
Ps. 67; 72 alt. Ps. 119. 33–56 Deut. ch. 6 Eph. 2. 1–10	W		Exod. ch. 24 Luke 1. 39–56	Deut. ch. 6 Eph. 2. 1–10
Ps. 73 alt. Ps. 39; 40 Deut. 7. 1–11 Eph. 2. 11–end	Wr	Alphege, Archbishop of Canterbury, Martyr, 1012 Com. Martyr	Exod. 25. 1–22 Luke 1. 57–end	Deut. 7. 1–11 Eph. 2. 11–end
Ps. 77 alt. Ps. 35 Deut. 7. 12–end Eph. 3. 1–13	W		Exod. 28. 1–4a, 29–38 Luke 2. 1–20	Deut. 7. 12–end Eph. 3. 1–13
Ps. 23; 27 alt. Ps. 45; 46 Deut. ch. 8 Eph. 3. 14–end ct	W		Exod. 29. 1–9 Luke 2. 21–40	Deut. ch. 8 Eph. 3. 14–end ct
Ps. 81. 8–16 Exod. 16. 4–15 Rev. 2. 12–17 Gospel: John 6. 30–40 or First EP of George Ps. 111; 116 Jer. 15. 15–end Heb. 11.32 – 12.2 R ct	W	THE THIRD SUNDAY AFTER EASTER Gen. 45. 3–10 Ps. 57 1 Pet. 2. 11–17 John 16. 16–22	Ps. 119. 89–96 Neh. 7.73b – 8.12 Luke 24. 25–32	Ps. 81. 8–16 Exod. 16. 4–15 Rev. 2. 12–17
EP: Ps. 3; 11 Isa. 43. 1–7 John 15. 1–8	Wr	George, Martyr, Patron of England, c. 304 To celebrate George, see Common Worship provision. Com. Martyr	Exod. 32. 1–14 Luke 2. 41–end	Deut. 9. 1–21 Eph. 4. 1–16

April 2018

			Sunday Principal Service Weekday Eucharist	Third Service Morning Prayer

24 Tu *Mellitus, Bishop of London, first Bishop at St Paul's, 624; The Seven Martyrs of the Melanesian Brotherhood,*
Solomon Islands, 2003

Acts 11. 19–26
Ps. 87
John 10. 22–30

Ps. 139
alt. Ps. *48*; 52
Exod. 32. 15–34
Luke 3. 1–14

W

25 W   MARK THE EVANGELIST

Prov. 15. 28–end
or Acts 15. 35–end
Ps. 119. 9–16
Eph. 4. 7–16
R   Mark 13. 5–13

MP: Ps. 37. 23–end; 148
Isa. 62. 6–10
or Ecclus. 51. 13–end
Acts 12.25 – 13.13

26 Th

Acts 13. 13–25
Ps. 89. 1–2, 20–26
John 13. 16–20

Ps. 118
alt. Ps. 56; *57*; (63†)
Exod. 34. 1–10, 27–end
W   Luke 4. 1–13

27 F   *Christina Rossetti, Poet, 1894*

Acts 13. 26–33
Ps. 2
John 14. 1–6

Ps. 33
alt. Ps. *51*; 54
Exod. 35.20 – 36.7
W   Luke 4. 14–30

28 Sa *Peter Chanel, Missionary in the South Pacific, Martyr, 1841*

Acts 13. 44–end
Ps. 98. 1–5
John 14. 7–14

Ps. 34
alt. Ps. 68
Exod. 40. 17–end
W   Luke 4. 31–37

29 S   THE FIFTH SUNDAY OF EASTER
The reading from Acts must be used
as either the first or second reading
at the Principal Service.

Acts 8. 26–end
[Baruch 3.9–15, 32 – 4.4
or Gen. 22. 1–18]
Ps. 22. 25–end
1 John 4. 7–end
W   John 15. 1–8

Ps. 44. 16–end
2 Macc. 7. 7–14
or Dan. 3. 16–28
Heb. 11.32 – 12.2

30 M   *Pandita Mary Ramabai, Translator of the Scriptures, 1922*

Acts 14. 5–18
Ps. 118. 1–3, 14–15
John 14. 21–26

Ps. 145
alt. Ps. 71
Num. 9. 15–end;
10. 33–end
Luke 4. 38–end

W

May 2018

1 Tu PHILIP AND JAMES, APOSTLES

Isa. 30. 15–21
Ps. 119. 1–8
Eph. 1. 3–10
R   John 14. 1–14

MP: Ps. 139; 146
Prov. 4. 10–18
James 1. 1–12

2 W   **Athanasius, Bishop of Alexandria, Teacher, 373**
Com. Teacher   *or*   Acts 15. 1–6
also Ecclus. 4. 20–28   Ps. 122. 1–5
Matt. 10. 24–27   John 15. 1–8
W

Ps. *30*; 147. 13–end
alt. Ps. 77
Num. ch. 12
Luke 5. 12–26

Second Service Evening Prayer	Calendar and Holy Communion	Morning Prayer	Evening Prayer
Ps. 115; *116* *alt*. Ps. 50 Deut. 9.23 – 10.5 Eph. 4. 17–end *or First EP of Mark* Ps. 19 Isa. 52. 7–10 Mark 1. 1–15 **R** ct	**W**	Exod. 32. 15–34 Luke 3. 1–14	Deut. 9.23 – 10.5 Eph. 4. 17–end *or First EP of Mark* (Ps. 19) Isa. 52. 7–10 Mark 1. 1–15 **R** ct
EP: Ps. 45 Ezek. 1. 4–14 2 Tim. 4. 1–11	MARK THE EVANGELIST Prov. 15. 28–end Ps. 119. 9–16 Eph. 4. 7–16 John 15. 1–11 **R**	(Ps. 37. 23–end; 148) Isa. 62. 6–10 *or* Ecclus. 51. 13–end Acts 12.25 – 13.13	(Ps. 45) Ezek. 1. 4–14 2 Tim. 4. 1–11
Ps. 81; *85* *alt*. Ps. 61; *62*; 64 Deut. 11. 8–end Eph. 5. 15–end	**W**	Exod. 34. 1–10, 27–end Luke 4. 1–13	Deut. 11. 8–end Eph. 5. 15–end
Ps. *36*; 40 *alt*. Ps. 38 Deut. 12. 1–14 Eph. 6. 1–9	**W**	Exod. 35.20 – 36.7 Luke 4. 14–30	Deut. 12. 1–14 Eph. 6. 1–9
Ps. *84*; 86 *alt*. Ps. 65; *66* Deut. 15. 1–18 Eph. 6. 10–end ct	**W**	Exod. 40. 17–end Luke 4. 31–37	Deut. 15. 1–18 Eph. 6. 10–end ct
Ps. 96 Isa. 60. 1–14 Rev. 3. 1–13 *Gospel*: Mark 16. 9–16	THE FOURTH SUNDAY AFTER EASTER Job 19. 21–27a Ps. 66. 14–end James 1. 17–21 John 16. 5–15 **W**	Ps. 44. 15–end 2 Macc. 7. 7–14 *or* Dan. 3. 16–28 Heb. 11.32 – 12.2	Ps. 96 Isa. 60. 1–14 Rev. 3. 1–13
Ps. 105 *alt*. Ps. *72*; 75 Deut. 16. 1–20 1 Pet. 1. 1–12 *or First EP of Philip and James* Ps. 25 Isa. 40. 27–end John 12. 20–26 **R** ct	**W**	Num. 9. 15–end; 10. 33–end Luke 4. 38–end	Deut. 16. 1–20 1 Pet. 1. 1–12 *or First EP of Philip and James* (Ps. 119. 1–8) Isa. 40. 27–end John 12. 20–26 **R** ct
EP: Ps. 149 Job 23. 1–12 John 1. 43–end	PHILIP AND JAMES, APOSTLES Prov. 4. 10–18 Ps. 25. 1–9 James 1. [1] 2–12 John 14. 1–14 **R**	(Ps. 139; 146) Isa. 30. 1–5 John 12. 20–26	(Ps. 149) Job 23. 1–12 John 1. 43–end
Ps. 98; *99*; 100 *alt*. Ps. 119. 81–104 Deut. 18. 9–end 1 Pet. 2. 1–10	**W**	Num. ch. 12 Luke 5. 12–26	Deut. 18. 9–end 1 Pet. 2. 1–10

May 2018

			Sunday Principal Service Weekday Eucharist	Third Service Morning Prayer
3	Th W		Acts 15. 7–21 Ps. 96. 1–3, 7–10 John 15. 9–11	Ps. **57**; 148 alt. Ps. 78. 1–39† Num. 13. 1–3, 17–end Luke 5. 27–end
4	F W	**English Saints and Martyrs of the Reformation Era** Isa. 43. 1–7 or or Ecclus. 2. 10–17 Ps. 87 2 Cor. 4. 5–12 John 12. 20–26	Acts 15. 22–31 Ps. 57. 8–end John 15. 12–17	Ps. **138**; 149 alt. Ps. 55 Num. 14. 1–25 Luke 6. 1–11
5	Sa W		Acts 16. 1–10 Ps. 100 John 15. 18–21	Ps. **146**; 150 alt. Ps. **76**; 79 Num. 14. 26–end Luke 6. 12–26
6	S W	THE SIXTH SUNDAY OF EASTER *The reading from Acts must be used as either the first or second reading at the Principal Service.*	Acts 10. 44–end [Isa. 55. 1–11] Ps. 98 1 John 5. 1–6 John 15. 9–17	Ps. 104. 26–32 Ezek. 47. 1–12 John 21. 1–19
7	M W	Rogation Day*	Acts 16. 11–15 Ps. 149. 1–5 John 15.26 – 16.4	Ps. **65**; 67 alt. Ps. **80**; 82 Num. 16. 1–35 Luke 6. 27–38
8	Tu W	**Julian of Norwich, Spiritual Writer, c. 1417** Rogation Day* Com. Religious or also 1 Cor. 13. 8–end Matt. 5. 13–16	Acts 16. 22–34 Ps. 138 John 16. 5–11	Ps. 124; 125; **126**; 127 alt. Ps. 87; **89. 1–18** Num. 16. 36–end Luke 6. 39–end
9	W W	Rogation Day*	Acts 17.15, 22 – 18.1 Ps. 148. 1–2, 11–end John 16. 12–15	Ps. **132**; 133 alt. Ps. 119. 105–128 Num. 17. 1–11 Luke 7. 1–10
10	Th W	**ASCENSION DAY** *The reading from Acts must be used as either the first or second reading at the Eucharist.*	Acts 1. 1–11 or Dan. 7. 9–14 Ps. 47 or Ps. 93 Eph. 1. 15–end or Acts 1. 1–11 Luke 24. 44–end	MP: Ps. 110; 150 Isa. 52. 7–end Heb. 7. [11–25] 26–end
11	F W		Acts 18. 9–18 Ps. 47. 1–6 John 16. 20–23	Ps. 20; **81** alt. Ps. **88**; (95) Num. 20. 1–13 Luke 7. 11–17 [Exod. 35.30 – 36.1 Gal. 5. 13–end]**
12	Sa W	Gregory Dix, Priest, Monk, Scholar, 1952	Acts 18. 22–end Ps. 47. 1–2, 7–end John 16. 23–28	Ps. 21; **47** alt. Ps. 96; **97**; 100 Num. 21. 4–9 Luke 7. 18–35 [Num. 11. 16–17, 24–29 1 Cor. ch. 2]**

*For Rogation Day provision, see p. 10.
**The alternative readings in square brackets may be used at one of the offices, in preparation for the Day of Pentecost.

Second Service Evening Prayer	Calendar and Holy Communion		Morning Prayer	Evening Prayer
	The Invention of the Cross		Num. 13. 1–3, 17–end	Deut. ch. 19
Ps. 104			Luke 5. 27–end	1 Pet. 2. 11–end
alt. Ps. 78. 40–end†				
Deut. ch. 19				
1 Pet. 2. 11–end		Wr		
Ps. 66			Num. 14. 1–25	Deut. 21.22 – 22.8
alt. Ps. 69			Luke 6. 1–11	1 Pet. 3. 1–12
Deut. 21.22 – 22.8				
1 Pet. 3. 1–12		W		
Ps. 118			Num. 14. 26–end	Deut. 24. 5–end
alt. Ps. 81; 84			Luke 6. 12–26	1 Pet. 3. 13–end
Deut. 24. 5–end				
1 Pet. 3. 13–end				
ct		W		ct
	THE FIFTH SUNDAY AFTER EASTER		Ps. 104. 26–32	Ps. 45
Ps. 45	Rogation Sunday		Ezek. 47. 1–12	Song of Sol.
Song of Sol. 4.16 – 5.2;	Joel 2. 21–26		John 21. 1–19	4.16 – 5.2; 8. 6–7
8. 6–7	Ps. 66. 1–8			Rev. 3. 14–end
Rev. 3. 14–end	James 1. 22–end			
Gospel: Luke 22. 24–30	John 16. 23b–end	W		
	Rogation Day			
Ps. 121; 122; 123	Job 28. 1–11		Num. 16. 1–35	Deut. ch. 26
alt. Ps. 85; 86	Ps. 107. 1–9		Luke 6. 27–38	1 Pet. 4. 1–11
Deut. ch. 26	James 5. 7–11			
1 Pet. 4. 1–11	Luke 6. 36–42	W		
	Rogation Day			
Ps. 128; 129; 130; 131	Deut. 8. 1–10		Num. 16. 36–end	Deut. 28. 1–14
alt. Ps. 89. 19–end	Ps. 121		Luke 6. 39–end	1 Pet. 4. 12–end
Deut. 28. 1–14	James 5. 16–end			
1 Pet. 4. 12–end	Luke 11. 5–13	W		
	Rogation Day			
First EP of Ascension Day	Deut. 34. 1–7		Num. 17. 1–11	First EP of
Ps. 15; 24	Ps. 108. 1–6		Luke 7. 1–10	Ascension Day
2 Sam. 23. 1–5	Eph. 4. 7–13			Ps. 15; 24
Col. 2.20 – 3.4	John 17. 1–11			2 Sam. 23. 1–5
				Col. 2.20 – 3.4
𝖂 ct		W		𝖂 ct
	ASCENSION DAY		Ps. 110; 150	Ps. 8
EP: Ps. 8	Dan. 7. 13–14		Isa. 52. 7–end	Song of the Three
Song of the Three 29–37	Ps. 68. 1–6		Heb. 7. [11–25] 26–end	29–37
or 2 Kings 2. 1–15	Acts 1. 1–11			or 2 Kings 2. 1–15
Rev. ch. 5	Mark 16. 14–end			Rev. ch. 5
Gospel: Matt. 28. 16–end	or Luke 24. 44–end	𝖂		
Ps. 145	Ascension CEG		Num. 20. 1–13	Deut. 29. 2–15
alt. Ps. 102			Luke 7. 11–17	1 John 1.1 – 2.6
Deut. 29. 2–15			[Exod. 35.30 – 36.1	
1 John 1.1 – 2.6			Gal. 5. 13–end]**	
		W		
	Ascension CEG		Num. 21. 4–9	Deut. ch. 30
Ps. 84; 85			Luke 7. 18–35	1 John 2. 7–17
alt. Ps. 104			[Num. 11. 16–17, 24–29	
Deut. ch. 30			1 Cor. ch. 2]**	
1 John 2. 7–17				
ct		W		ct

May 2018

		Sunday Principal Service Weekday Eucharist	Third Service Morning Prayer

13 S — THE SEVENTH SUNDAY OF EASTER (SUNDAY AFTER ASCENSION DAY)

The reading from Acts must be used as either the first or second reading at the Principal Service.

	Acts 1. 15–17, 21–end	Ps. 76
	[Ezek. 36. 24–28]	Isa. 14. 3–15
	Ps. 1	Rev. 14. 1–13
	1 John 5. 9–13	
	John 17. 6–19	

W

14 M — MATTHIAS THE APOSTLE*

	Isa. 22. 15–end	MP: Ps. 16; 147. 1–12
	or Acts 1. 15–end	1 Sam. 2. 27–35
	Ps. 15	Acts 2. 37–end
	Acts 1. 15–end	
R	or 1 Cor. 4. 1–7	
	John 15. 9–17	

or, if Matthias is celebrated on 24 February:

	Acts 19. 1–8	Ps. 93; 96; 97
	Ps. 68. 1–6	alt. Ps. 98; 99; 101
	John 16. 29–end	Num. 22. 1–35
		Luke 7. 36–end
W		[Num. 27. 15–end
		1 Cor. ch. 3]**

15 Tu

	Acts 20. 17–27	Ps. 98; 99; 100
	Ps. 68. 9–10, 18–19	alt. Ps. 106† (or 103)
	John 17. 1–11	Num. 22.36 – 23.12
		Luke 8. 1–15
W		[1 Sam. 10. 1–10
		1 Cor. 12. 1–13]**

16 W — Caroline Chisholm, Social Reformer, 1877

	Acts 20. 28–end	Ps. 2; 29
	Ps. 68. 27–28, 32–end	alt. Ps. 110; 111; 112
	John 17. 11–19	Num. 23. 13–end
		Luke 8. 16–25
W		[1 Kings 19. 1–18
		Matt. 3. 13–end]**

17 Th

	Acts 22. 30; 23. 6–11	Ps. 24; 72
	Ps. 16. 1, 5–end	alt. Ps. 113; 115
	John 17. 20–end	Num. ch. 24
		Luke 8. 26–39
W		[Ezek. 11. 14–20
		Matt. 9.35 – 10.20]**

18 F

	Acts 25. 13–21	Ps. 28; 30
	Ps. 103. 1–2, 11–12, 19–20	alt. Ps. 139
	John 21. 15–19	Num. 27. 12–end
		Luke 8. 40–end
W		[Ezek. 36. 22–28
		Matt. 12. 22–32]**

19 Sa — **Dunstan, Archbishop of Canterbury, Restorer of Monastic Life, 988**

Com. Bishop	or	Acts 28. 16–20, 30–end	Ps. 42; 43
esp. Matt. 24. 42–46		Ps. 11. 4–end	alt. Ps. 120; 121; 122
also Exod. 31. 1–5		John 21. 20–end	Num. 32. 1–27
			Luke 9. 1–17
W			[Mic. 3. 1–8
			Eph. 6. 10–20]**

20 S — **DAY OF PENTECOST (Whit Sunday)**

The reading from Acts must be used as either the first or second reading at the Principal Service.

	Acts 2. 1–21	MP: Ps. 145
	or Ezek. 37. 1–14	Isa. 11. 1–9
	Ps. 104. 26–36, 37b (or 26–end)	or Wisd. 7. 15–23 [24–27]
	Rom. 8. 22–27	1 Cor. 12. 4–13
	or Acts 2. 1–21	
R	John 15. 26–27; 16. 4b–15	

*Matthias may be celebrated on 24 February instead of 14 May.
**The alternative readings in square brackets may be used at one of the offices, in preparation for the Day of Pentecost.

Second Service Evening Prayer		Calendar and Holy Communion	Morning Prayer	Evening Prayer
		THE SUNDAY AFTER ASCENSION DAY		
Ps. 147. 1–12		2 Kings 2. 9–15	Ps. 76	Ps. 147. 1–12
Isa. ch. 61		Ps. 68. 32–end	Isa. 14. 3–15	Isa. ch. 61
Luke 4. 14–21		1 Pet. 4. 7–11	Rev. 14. 1–13	Luke 4. 14–21
or First EP of Matthias		John 15.26 – 16.4a		
Ps. 147				
Isa. 22. 15–22				
Phil. 3.13b – 4.1				
R ct	W			
EP: Ps. 80			Num. 22. 1–35	Deut. 31. 1–13
1 Sam. 16. 1–13a			Luke 7. 36–end	1 John 2. 18–end
Matt. 7. 15–27			[Num. 27. 15–end	
			1 Cor. ch. 3]**	
Ps. 18				
alt. Ps. **105**† (or 103)				
Deut. 31. 1–13				
1 John 2. 18–end				
	W			
Ps. 68			Num. 22.36 – 23.12	Deut. 31. 14–29
alt. Ps. 107†			Luke 8. 1–15	1 John 3. 1–10
Deut. 31. 14–29			[1 Sam. 10. 1–10	
1 John 3. 1–10			1 Cor. 12. 1–13]**	
	W			
Ps. 36; **46**			Num. 23. 13–end	Deut. 31.30 – 32.14
alt. Ps. 119. 129–152			Luke 8. 16–25	1 John 3. 11–end
Deut. 31.30 – 32.14			[1 Kings 19. 1–18	
1 John 3. 11–end			Matt. 3. 13–end]**	
	W			
Ps. 139			Num. ch. 24	Deut. 32. 15–47
alt. Ps. 114; **116**; 117			Luke 8. 26–39	1 John 4. 1–6
Deut. 32. 15–47			[Ezek. 11. 14–20	
1 John 4. 1–6			Matt. 9.35 – 10.20]**	
	W			
Ps. 147			Num. 27. 12–end	Deut. ch. 33
alt. Ps. **130**; 131; 137			Luke 8. 40–end	1 John 4. 7–end
Deut. ch. 33			[Ezek. 36. 22–28	
1 John 4. 7–end			Matt. 12. 22–32]**	
	W			
		Dunstan, Archbishop of Canterbury, Restorer of Monastic Life, 988		
First EP of Pentecost		Com. Bishop	Num. 32. 1–27	*First EP of Pentecost*
Ps. 48			Luke 9. 1–17	Ps. 48
Deut. 16. 9–15			[Mic. 3. 1–8	Deut. 16. 9–15
John 7. 37–39			Eph. 6. 10–20]**	John 7. 37–39
R ct	W			**R ct**
		WHIT SUNDAY		
EP: Ps. 139. 1–11, 13–18,		Deut. 16. 9–12	Ps. 145	Ps. 139. 1–11, 13–18,
23–24 (or 139. 1–11)		Ps. 122	Isa. 11. 1–9	23–24 (or 139. 1–11)
Ezek. 36. 22–28		Acts 2. 1–11	*or* Wisd. 7. 15–23	Ezek. 36. 22–28
Acts 2. 22–38		John 14. 15–31a	[24–27]	Acts 2. 22–38
Gospel: John 20. 19–23			1 Cor. 12. 4–13	
	R			

May 2018

			Sunday Principal Service Weekday Eucharist	Third Service Morning Prayer

21
DEL 7

M · Helena, Protector of the Holy Places, 330
Ordinary Time resumes today

G

James 3. 13–end
Ps. 19. 7–end
Mark 9. 14–29

Ps. 123; 124; 125; *126*
Josh. ch. 1
Luke 9. 18–27

22

Tu

G

James 4. 1–10
Ps. 55. 7–9, 24
Mark 9. 30–37

Ps. *132*; 133
Josh. ch. 2
Luke 9. 28–36

23

W

G

James 4. 13–end
Ps. 49. 1–2, 5–10
Mark 9. 38–40

Ps. 119. 153–end
Josh. ch. 3
Luke 9. 37–50

24

Th · **John and Charles Wesley, Evangelists, Hymn Writers, 1791 and 1788**
Com. Pastor   *or*
also Eph. 5. 15–20

Gw

James 5. 1–6
Ps. 49. 12–20
Mark 9. 41–50

Ps. *143*; 146
Josh. 4.1 – 5.1
Luke 9. 51–end

25

F · **The Venerable Bede, Monk at Jarrow, Scholar, Historian, 735**
Aldhelm, Bishop of Sherborne, 709
Com. Religious   *or*
also Ecclus. 39. 1–10

Gw

James 5. 9–12
Ps. 103. 1–4, 8–13
Mark 10. 1–12

Ps. *142*; 144
Josh. 5. 2–end
Luke 10. 1–16

26

Sa · **Augustine, first Archbishop of Canterbury, 605**
John Calvin, Reformer, 1564; Philip Neri, Founder of the Oratorians, Spiritual Guide, 1595
Com. Bishop   *or*
also 1 Thess. 2. 2b–8
Matt. 13. 31–33

James 5. 13–end
Ps. 141. 1–4
Mark 10. 13–16

Ps. 147
Josh. 6. 1–20
Luke 10. 17–24

Gw

27

S · **TRINITY SUNDAY**

𝇩

Isa. 6. 1–8
Ps. 29
Rom. 8. 12–17
John 3. 1–17

MP: Ps. 33. 1–12
Prov. 8. 1–4, 22–31
2 Cor. 13. [5–10] 11–end

28
DEL 8

M · Lanfranc, Prior of Le Bec, Archbishop of Canterbury, Scholar, 1089

G

1 Pet. 1. 3–9
Ps. 111
Mark 10. 17–27

Ps. *1*: 2; 3
Josh. 7. 1–15
Luke 10. 25–37

29

Tu

G

1 Pet. 1. 10–16
Ps. 98. 1–5
Mark 10. 28–31

Ps. *5*; 6; (8)
Josh. 7. 16–end
Luke 10. 38–end

30

W · **Josephine Butler, Social Reformer, 1906**
Joan of Arc, Visionary, 1431; Apolo Kivebulaya, Evangelist in Central Africa, 1933
Com. Saint   *or*
esp. Isa. 58. 6–11
also 1 John 3. 18–23
Matt. 9. 10–13

1 Pet. 1. 18–end
Ps. 147. 13–end
Mark 10. 32–45

Ps. 119. 1–32
Josh. 8. 1–29
Luke 11. 1–13

Gw

Second Service Evening Prayer	Calendar and Holy Communion		Morning Prayer	Evening Prayer
Ps. *127*; 128; 129 2 Chron. 17. 1–12 Rom. 1. 1–17	**Monday in Whitsun Week** Acts 10. 34–end John 3. 16–21	R	Ezek. 11. 14–20 Acts 2. 12–36	Exod. 35.30 – 36.1 Acts 2. 37–end
Ps. (134); *1* 2 Chron. 1 Rom. 1. 18 end	**Tuesday in Whitsun Week** Acts 8. 14–17 John 10. 1–10	R	Ezek. 37. 1–14 1 Cor. 12. 1–13	2 Sam. 23. 1–5 1 Cor. 12.27 – 13.end
Ps. 136 2 Chron. 18.2? 19.end Rom. 2. 1–16	Ember Day Ember CEG *or* Acts 2. 14–21 John 6. 44–51	R	Josh. ch. 3 Luke 9. 37–50	2 Chron. 18.28 – 19.end Rom. 2. 1–16
Ps. *138*; 140; 141 2 Chron. 20. 1–23 Rom. 2. 17–end	Acts 2. 22–28 Luke 9. 1–6	R	Josh. 4.1 – 5.1 Luke 9. 51–end	2 Chron. 20. 1–23 Rom. 2. 17–end
Ps. 145 2 Chron. 22.10 – 23.end Rom. 3. 1–20	Ember Day Ember CEG *or* Acts 8. 5–8 Luke 5. 17–26	R	Josh. 5. 2–end Luke 10. 1–16	2 Chron. 22.10 – 23.end Rom. 3. 1–20
First EP of Trinity Sunday Ps. 97; 98 Isa. 40. 12–end Mark 1. 1–13 *W* ct	**Augustine, first Archbishop of Canterbury, 605** Ember Day Com. Bishop *or* Ember CEG *or* Acts 13. 44–end Matt. 20. 29–end	Rw	Josh. 6. 1–20 Luke 10. 17–24	*First EP of Trinity Sunday* Ps. 97; 98 Isa. 40. 12–end Mark 1. 1–13 *W* ct
EP: Ps. 104. 1–10 Ezek. 1. 4–10, 22–28a Rev. ch. 4 *Gospel:* Mark 1. 1–13	**TRINITY SUNDAY** Isa. 6. 1–8 Ps. 8 Rev. 4. 1–11 John 3. 1–15	*W*	Ps. 33. 1–12 Prov. 8. 1–4, 22–31 2 Cor. 13. [5–10] 11–end	Ps. 104. 1–10 Ezek. 1. 4–10, 22–28a Mark 1. 1–13
Ps. *4*; 7 2 Chron. 26. 1–21 Rom. 4. 1–12		G	Josh. 7. 1–15 Luke 10. 25–37	2 Chron. 26. 1–21 Rom. 4. 1–12
Ps. *9*; 10† 2 Chron. ch. 28 Rom. 4. 13–end		G	Josh. 7. 16–end Luke 10. 38–end	2 Chron. ch. 28 Rom. 4. 13–end
Ps. *11*; 12; 13 2 Chron. 29. 1–19 Rom. 5. 1–11 *or First EP of Corpus Christi* Ps. 110; 111 Exod. 16. 2–15 John 6. 22–35 **W** ct *or First EP of the Visit of* *Mary to Elizabeth* Ps. 45 Song of Sol. 2. 8–14 Luke 1. 26–38 **W** ct		G	Josh. 8. 1–29 Luke 11. 1–13	2 Chron. 29. 1–19 Rom. 5. 1–11

May 2018

		Sunday Principal Service Weekday Eucharist	Third Service Morning Prayer

31

Th	DAY OF THANKSGIVING FOR HOLY COMMUNION (CORPUS CHRISTI)		
		Gen. 14. 18–20	MP: Ps. 147
		Ps. 116. 10–end	Deut. 8. 2–16
		I Cor. 11. 23–26	I Cor. 10. 1–17
W		John 6. 51–58	
Or:	THE VISIT OF THE BLESSED VIRGIN MARY TO ELIZABETH*		
	(or transferred to 1 June if Corpus Christi is celebrated as a Festival)		
		Zeph. 3. 14–18	MP: Ps. 85; 150
		Ps. 113	1 Sam. 2. 1–10
		Rom. 12. 9–16	Mark 3. 31–end
W		Luke 1. 39–49 [50–56]	
	or, if kept as a feria and The Visitation is celebrated on 2 July:		
		1 Pet. 2. 2–5, 9–12	Ps. 14; 15; 16
		Ps. 100	Josh. 8. 30–end
G		Mark 10. 46–end	Luke 11. 14–28

June 2018

1

F	Justin, Martyr at Rome, c. 165			
	Com. Martyr	or	1 Pet. 4. 7–13	Ps. 17; 19
	esp. John 15. 18–21		Ps. 96. 10–end	Josh. 9. 3–26
	also 1 Macc. 2. 15–22		Mark 11. 11–26	Luke 11. 29–36
Gr	1 Cor. 1. 18–25			

2

Sa		Jude 17, 20–end	Ps. 20; 21; 23
		Ps. 63. 1–6	Josh. 10. 1–15
G		Mark 11. 27–end	Luke 11. 37–end

3

S	THE FIRST SUNDAY AFTER TRINITY (Proper 4)		
	Track 1	Track 2	
	1 Sam. 3. 1–10 [11–20]	Deut. 5. 12–15	Ps. 28; 32
	Ps. 139. 1–5, 12–18	Ps. 81. 1–10	Deut. 5. 1–21
	2 Cor. 4. 5–12	2 Cor. 4. 5–12	Acts 21. 17–39a
G	Mark 2.23 – 3.6	Mark 2.23 – 3.6	

4
DEL 9

M	Petroc, Abbot of Padstow, 6th century		
		2 Pet. 1. 2–7	Ps. 27; 30
		Ps. 91. 1–2, 14–end	Josh. ch. 14
G		Mark 12. 1–12	Luke 12. 1–12

5

Tu	Boniface (Wynfrith) of Crediton, Bishop, Apostle of Germany, Martyr, 754			
	Com. Martyr	or	2 Pet. 3. 11–15a, 17–end	Ps. 32; 36
	also Acts 20. 24–28		Ps. 90. 1–4, 10, 14, 16	Josh. 21.43 – 22.8
Gr			Mark 12. 13–17	Luke 12. 13–21

6

W	Ini Kopuria, Founder of the Melanesian Brotherhood, 1945		
		2 Tim. 1. 1–3, 6–12	Ps. 34
		Ps. 123	Josh. 22. 9–end
G		Mark 12. 18–27	Luke 12. 22–31

7

Th		2 Tim. 2. 8–15	Ps. 37†
		Ps. 25. 4–12	Josh. ch. 23
G		Mark 12. 28–34	Luke 12. 32–40

8

F	Thomas Ken, Bishop of Bath and Wells, Nonjuror, Hymn Writer, 1711			
	Com. Bishop	or	2 Tim. 3. 10–end	Ps. 31
	esp. 2 Cor. 4. 1–10		Ps. 119. 161–168	Josh. 24. 1–28
Gw	Matt. 24. 42–46		Mark 12. 35–37	Luke 12. 41–48

9

Sa	Columba, Abbot of Iona, Missionary, 597			
	Ephrem of Syria, Deacon, Hymn Writer, Teacher, 373			
	Com. Missionary	or	2 Tim. 4. 1–8	Ps. 41; 42; 43
	also Titus 2. 11–end		Ps. 71. 7–16	Josh. 24. 29–end
Gw			Mark 12. 38–end	Luke 12. 49–end

*The Visit of the Blessed Virgin Mary to Elizabeth may be celebrated on 2 July instead of 31 May.

Second Service Evening Prayer		Calendar and Holy Communion	Morning Prayer	Evening Prayer
		To celebrate Corpus Christi, see *Common Worship* provision.		
EP: Ps. 23; 42; 43 Prov. 9. 1–5 Luke 9. 11–17			Josh. 8. 30–end Luke 11. 14–28	2 Chron. 29. 20–end Rom. 5. 12–end
EP: Ps. 122; 127; 128 Zech. 2. 10–end John 3. 25–30				
Ps. 18† 2 Chron. 29. 20–end Rom. 5. 12–end	G			
Ps. 22 2 Chron. ch. 30 Rom. 6. 1–14	Gr	**Nicomede, Priest and Martyr at Rome (date unknown)** Com. Martyr	Josh. 9. 3–26 Luke 11. 29–36	2 Chron. ch. 30 Rom. 6. 1–14
Ps. *24*; 25 2 Chron. 32. 1–22 Rom. 6. 15–end ct	G		Josh. 10. 1–15 Luke 11. 37–end	2 Chron. 32. 1–22 Rom. 6. 15–end ct
Ps. 35 (*or* 35. 1–10) Jer. 5. 1–19 Rom. 7. 7–end Gospel: Luke 7. 1–10	G	**THE FIRST SUNDAY AFTER TRINITY** 2 Sam. 9. 6–end Ps. 41. 1–4 1 John 4. 7–end Luke 16. 19–31	Ps. 28; 32 Deut. 5. 1–21 Acts 21. 17–39a	Ps. 35 (*or* 35. 1–10) Jer. 5. 1–19 Rom. 7. 7–end
Ps. 26; *28*; 29 2 Chron. 33. 1–13 Rom. 7. 1–6	G		Josh. ch. 14 Luke 12. 1–12	2 Chron. 33. 1–13 Rom. 7. 1–6
Ps. 33 2 Chron. 34. 1–18 Rom. 7. 7–end	Gr	**Boniface (Wynfrith) of Crediton, Bishop, Apostle of Germany, Martyr, 754** Com. Martyr	Josh. 21.43 – 22.8 Luke 12. 13–21	2 Chron. 34. 1–18 Rom. 7. 7–end
Ps. 119. 33–56 2 Chron. 34. 19–end Rom. 8. 1–11	G		Josh. 22. 9–end Luke 12. 22–31	2 Chron. 34. 19–end Rom. 8. 1–11
Ps. 39; *40* 2 Chron. 35. 1–19 Rom. 8. 12–17	G		Josh. ch. 23 Luke 12. 32–40	2 Chron. 35. 1–19 Rom. 8. 12–17
Ps. 35 2 Chron. 35.20 – 36.10 Rom. 8. 18–30	G		Josh. 24. 1–28 Luke 12. 41–48	2 Chron. 35.20 – 36.10 Rom. 8. 18–30
Ps. 45; *46* 2 Chron. 36. 11–end Rom. 8. 31–end ct	G		Josh. 24. 29–end Luke 12. 49–end	2 Chron. 36. 11–end Rom. 8. 31–end ct

June 2018

			Sunday Principal Service Weekday Eucharist	Third Service Morning Prayer
10	S	THE SECOND SUNDAY AFTER TRINITY **(Proper 5)**		
			Track 1	*Track 2*	
			1 Sam. 8. 4–11 [12–15] 16–20;	Gen. 3. 8–15	Ps. 36
			[11. 14–end]	Ps. 130	Deut. 6. 10–end
			Ps. 138	2 Cor. 4.13 – 5.1	Acts 22.22 – 23.11
			2 Cor. 4.13 – 5.1	Mark 3. 20–end	
			Mark 3. 20–end		
	G			
11 DEL 10	M	BARNABAS THE APOSTLE	Job 29. 11–16	MP: Ps. 100; 101; 117
			or Acts 11. 19–end	Jer. 9. 23–24
			Ps. 112	Acts 4. 32–end
			Acts 11. 19–end	
			or Gal. 2. 1–10	
	R		John 15. 12–17	
12	Tu		1 Kings. 17. 7–16	Ps. *48*; 52
			Ps. 4	Judg. 4. 1–23
	G		Matt. 5. 13–16	Luke 13. 10–21
13	W		1 Kings 18. 20–39	Ps. 119. 57–80
			Ps. 16. 1, 6–end	Judg. ch. 5
	G		Matt. 5. 17–19	Luke 13. 22–end
14	Th	*Richard Baxter, Puritan Divine, 1691*	1 Kings 18. 41–end	Ps. 56; *57*; (63†)
			Ps. 65. 8–end	Judg. 6. 1–24
	G		Matt. 5. 20–26	Luke 14. 1–11
15	F	*Evelyn Underhill, Spiritual Writer, 1941*	1 Kings 19. 9, 11–16	Ps. *51*; 54
			Ps. 27. 8–16	Judg. 6. 25–end
	G		Matt. 5. 27–32	Luke 14. 12–24
16	Sa	**Richard, Bishop of Chichester, 1253**		Ps. 68
		Joseph Butler, Bishop of Durham, Philosopher, 1752		
		Com. Bishop *or* 1 Kings 19. 19–end	Judg. ch. 7
		also John 21. 15–19 Ps. 16. 1–7	Luke 14. 25–end
			Matt. 5. 33–37	
	Gw			
17	S	THE THIRD SUNDAY AFTER TRINITY **(Proper 6)**		
			Track 1	*Track 2*	
			1 Sam. 15.34 – 16.13	Ezek. 17. 22–end	Ps. 42; 43
			Ps. 20	Ps. 92. 1–4, 12–end (*or* 1–8)	Deut. 10.12 – 11.1
			2 Cor. 5. 6–10 [11–13] 14–17	2 Cor. 5. 6–10 [11–13] 14–17	Acts 23. 12–35
	G		Mark 4. 26–34	Mark 4. 26–34	
18 DEL 11	M	*Bernard Mizeki, Apostle of the MaShona, Martyr, 1896*	1 Kings 21. 1–16	Ps. 71
			Ps. 5. 1–5	Judg. 8. 22–end
	G		Matt. 5. 38–42	Luke 15. 1–10
19	Tu	*Sundar Singh of India, Sadhu (holy man), Evangelist, Teacher, 1929*	1 Kings 21. 17–end	Ps. 73
			Ps. 51. 1–9	Judg. 9. 1–21
	G		Matt. 5. 43–end	Luke 15. 11–end
20	W		2 Kings 2. 1, 6–14	Ps. 77
			Ps. 31. 21–end	Judg. 9. 22–end
	G		Matt. 6. 1–6, 16–18	Luke 16. 1–18
21	Th		Ecclus. 48. 1–14	Ps. 78. 1–39†
			or Isa. 63. 7–9	Judg. 11. 1–11
			Ps. 97. 1–8	Luke 16. 19–end
	G		Matt. 6. 7–15	
22	F	**Alban, first Martyr of Britain, c. 250**		Ps. 55
		Com. Martyr *or* 2 Kings 11. 1–4, 9–18, 20	Judg. 11. 29–end
		esp. 2 Tim. 2. 3–13 Ps. 132. 1–5, 11–13	Luke 17. 1–10
	Gr	John 12. 24–26 Matt. 6. 19–23	

Second Service Evening Prayer	Calendar and Holy Communion		Morning Prayer	Evening Prayer
	THE SECOND SUNDAY AFTER TRINITY			
Ps. 37. 1–17 (or 37. 1–11) Jer. 6. 16–21 Rom. 9. 1–13 Gospel: Luke 7. 11–17 or First EP of Barnabas Ps. 1; 15 Isa. 42. 5–12 Acts 14. 8–end **R ct**	Gen. 12. 1–4 Ps. 120 1 John 3. 13–end Luke 14. 16–24	G	Ps. 36 Deut. 6. 10–end Acts 22.22 – 23.11	Ps. 37. 1–17 (or 37. 1–11) Jer. 6. 16–21 Rom. 9. 1–13 or First EP of Barnabas Ps. 1; 15 Isa. 42. 5–12 Acts 14. 8–end **R ct**
	BARNABAS THE APOSTLE			
EP: Ps. 147 Eccles. 12. 9–end or Tobit 4. 5–11 Acts 9. 26–31	Job 29. 11–16 Ps. 112 Acts 11. 22–end John 15. 12–16	R	(Ps. 100; 101; 117) Jer. 9. 23–24 Acts 4. 32–end	(Ps. 147) Eccles. 12. 9–end or Tobit 4. 5–11 Acts 9. 26–31
Ps. 50 Ezra ch. 3 Rom. 9. 19–end		G	Judg. 4. 1–23 Luke 13. 10–21	Ezra ch. 3 Rom. 9. 19–end
Ps. 59; 60; (67) Ezra 4. 1–5 Rom. 10. 1–10		G	Judg. ch. 5 Luke 13. 22–end	Ezra 4. 1–5 Rom. 10. 1–10
Ps. 61; 62; 64 Ezra 4. 7–end Rom. 10. 11–end		G	Judg. 6. 1–24 Luke 14. 1–11	Ezra 4. 7–end Rom. 10. 11–end
Ps. 38 Ezra ch. 5 Rom. 11. 1–12		G	Judg. 6. 25–end Luke 14. 12–24	Ezra ch. 5 Rom. 11. 1–12
Ps. 65; 66 Ezra ch. 6 Rom. 11. 13–24 ct		G	Judg. ch. 7 Luke 14. 25–end	Ezra ch. 6 Rom. 11. 13–24 ct
	THE THIRD SUNDAY AFTER TRINITY			
Ps. 39 Jer. 7. 1–16 Rom. 9. 14–26 Gospel: Luke 7.36 – 8.3	2 Chron. 33. 9–13 Ps. 55. 17–23 1 Pet. 5. 5b–11 Luke 15. 1–10	G	Ps. 42; 43 Deut. 10.12 – 11.1 Acts 23. 12–35	Ps. 39 Jer. 7. 1–16 Rom. 9. 14–26
Ps. 72; 75 Ezra ch. 7 Rom. 11. 25–end		G	Judg. 8. 22–end Luke 15. 1–10	Ezra ch. 7 Rom. 11. 25–end
Ps. 74 Ezra 8. 15–end Rom. 12. 1–8		G	Judg. 9. 1–21 Luke 15. 11–end	Ezra 8. 15–end Rom. 12. 1–8
	Translation of Edward, King of the West Saxons, 979 Com. Martyr			
Ps. 119. 81–104 Ezra ch. 9 Rom. 12. 9–end		Gr	Judg. 9. 22–end Luke 16. 1–18	Ezra ch. 9 Rom. 12. 9–end
Ps. 78. 40–end† Ezra 10. 1–17 Rom. 13. 1–7		G	Judg. 11. 1–11 Luke 16. 19–end	Ezra 10. 1–17 Rom. 13. 1–7
Ps. 69 Neh. ch. 1 Rom. 13. 8–end		G	Judg. 11. 29–end Luke 17. 1–10	Neh. ch. 1 Rom. 13. 8–end

June 2018

	Sunday Principal Service Weekday Eucharist	Third Service Morning Prayer

23 Sa **Etheldreda, Abbess of Ely, c. 678**
Com. Religious   or   2 Chron. 24. 17–25   Ps. **76**; 79
also Matt. 25. 1–13   Ps. 89. 25–33   Judg. 12. 1–7
                                               Matt. 6. 24–end   Luke 17. 11–19

Gw

24 S   THE BIRTH OF JOHN THE BAPTIST (or transferred to 25 June)
                                               Isa. 40. 1–11   MP: Ps. 50; 149
                                               Ps. 85. 7–end   Ecclus. 48. 1–10
                                               Acts 13. 14b–26   *or* Mal. 3. 1–6
                                               or Gal. 3. 23–end   Luke 3. 1–17
     W   Luke 1. 57–66, 80

or, for The Fourth Sunday after Trinity (Proper 7):
Track 1   Track 2
1 Sam. 17. [1a, 4–11, 19–23] 32–49   Job 38. 1–11   Ps. 48
and Ps. 9. 9–end   Ps. 107. 1–3, 23–32 (*or* 23–32)   Deut. 11. 1–15
or 1 Sam. 17.57 – 18.5, 10–16   2 Cor. 6. 1–13   Acts 27. 1–12
and Ps. 133   Mark 4. 35–end
2 Cor. 6. 1–13
     G   Mark 4. 35–end

25 M   2 Kings 17. 5–8, 13–15, 18   Ps. **80**; 82
DEL 12   G   Ps. 60. 1–5, 11–end   Judg. 13. 1–24
                                               Matt. 7. 1–5   Luke 17. 20–end

26 Tu   2 Kings 19. 9b–11,   Ps. 87; **89**. *1–18*
                                               14–21, 31–36   Judg. ch. 14
                                               Ps. 48. 1–2, 8–end   Luke 18. 1–14
     G   Matt. 7. 6, 12–14

27 W   Ember Day*
            Cyril, Bishop of Alexandria, Teacher, 444
                                               2 Kings 22. 8–13; 23. 1–3   Ps. 119. 105–128
                                               Ps. 119. 33–40   Judg. 15.1 – 16.3
     G or R   Matt. 7. 15–20   Luke 18. 15–30

28 Th   **Irenaeus, Bishop of Lyons, Teacher, c. 200**
            Com. Teacher   or 2 Kings 24. 8–17   Ps. 90; **92**
            also 2 Pet. 1. 16–end   Ps. 79. 1–9, 12   Judg. 16. 4–end
                                               Matt. 7. 21–end   Luke 18. 31–end

Gw

29 F   PETER AND PAUL, APOSTLES
            Ember Day*
                                               Zech. 4. 1–6a, 10b–end   MP: Ps. 71; 113
                                               or Acts 12. 1–11   Isa. 49. 1–6
                                               Ps. 125   Acts 11. 1–18
                                               Acts 12. 1–11
                                               or 2 Tim. 4. 6–8, 17–18
     R   Matt. 16. 13–19

or, if Peter is commemorated alone:
                                               Ezek. 3. 22–end   MP: Ps. 71; 113
                                               or Acts 12. 1–11   Isa. 49. 1–6
                                               Ps. 125   Acts 11. 1–18
                                               Acts 12. 1–11
                                               or 1 Pet. 2. 19–end
     R   Matt. 16. 13–19

*For Ember Day provision, see p. 11.

Second Service Evening Prayer	Calendar and Holy Communion	Morning Prayer	Evening Prayer
Ps. 81; *84* Neh. ch. 2 Rom. 14. 1–12 ct *or First EP of The Birth of John the Baptist* Ps. 71 Judges 13. 2–7, 24–end Luke 1. 5–25 **W ct**	**G**	Judg. 12. 1–7 Luke 17. 11–19	Neh. ch. 2 Rom. 14. 1–12 ct *or First EP of The Nativity of John the Baptist* (Ps. 71) Judges 13. 2–7, 24–end Luke 1. 5–25 **W ct**
EP: Ps. 80; 82 Mal. ch. 4 Matt. 11. 2–19	**THE NATIVITY OF JOHN THE BAPTIST** (or transferred to 25 June) Isa. 40. 1–11 Ps. 80. 1–7 Acts 13. 22–26 Luke 1. 57–80 **W** *or, for The Fourth Sunday after Trinity:*	Ps. 50; 149 Ecclus. 48. 1–10 or Mal. 3. 1–6 Luke 3. 1–17	Ps. 82 Mal. ch. 4 Matt. 11. 2–19
Ps. 49 Jer. 10. 1–16 Rom. 11. 25–end *Gospel*: Luke 8. 26–39	Gen. 3. 17–19 Ps. 79. 8–10 Rom. 8. 18–23 Luke 6. 36–42 **G**	Ps. 48 Deut. 11. 1–15 Acts 27. 1–12	Ps. 49 Jer. 10. 1–16 Rom. 11. 25–end
Ps. *85*; 86 Neh. ch. 4 Rom. 14. 13–end	**G**	Judg. 13. 1–24 Luke 17. 20–end	Neh. ch. 4 Rom. 14. 13–end
Ps. 89. 19–end Neh. ch. 5 Rom. 15. 1–13	**G**	Judg. ch. 14 Luke 18. 1–14	Neh. ch. 5 Rom. 15. 1–13
Ps. *91*; 93 Neh. 6.1 – 7.4 Rom. 15. 14–21	**G**	Judg. 15.1 – 16.3 Luke 18. 15–30	Neh. 6.1 – 7.4 Rom. 15. 14–21
Ps. 94 Neh. 7.73b – 8.end Rom. 15. 22–end *or First EP of Peter and Paul* Ps. 66; 67 Ezek. 3. 4–11 Gal. 1.13 – 2.8 *or, for Peter alone:* Acts 9. 32–end **R ct**	**G**	Judg. 16. 4–end Luke 18. 31–end	Neh. 7.73b – 8.end Rom. 15. 22–end *or First EP of Peter* (Ps. 66; 67) Ezek. 3. 4–11 Acts 9. 32–end **R ct**
EP: Ps. 124; 138 Ezek. 34. 11–16 John 21. 15–22	**PETER THE APOSTLE** Ezek. 3. 4–11 Ps. 125 Acts 12. 1–11 Matt. 16. 13–19	(Ps. 71; 113) Isa. 49. 1–6 Acts 11. 1–18	(Ps. 124; 138) Ezek. 34. 11–16 John 21. 15–22
EP: Ps. 124; 138 Ezek. 34. 11–16 John 21. 15–22	**R**		

June 2018

		Sunday Principal Service Weekday Eucharist	Third Service Morning Prayer

30	Sa	Ember Day*	Lam. 2. 2, 10–14, 18–19 Ps. 74. 1–3, 21–end Matt. 8. 5–17	Ps. 96; **97**; 100 Judg. 18. 1–20, 27–end Luke 19. 11–27
	G or R			

July 2018

1	S	**THE FIFTH SUNDAY AFTER TRINITY (Proper 8)**		
		Track 1 1 Sam. 1. 1, 17–end Ps. 130 2 Cor. 8. 7–end Mark 5. 21–end	*Track 2* Wisd. of Sol. 1. 13–15; 2. 23–24 Ps. 56 *Canticle:* Lam. 3. 22–33 *or* Ps. 30 2 Cor. 8. 7–end Mark 5. 21–end	Deut. 15. 1–11 Acts 27. [13–32] 33–end
	G			

2 DEL 13	M	**	Amos 2. 6–10, 13–end Ps. 50. 16–23 Matt. 8. 18–22	Ps. **98**; 99; 101 1 Sam. 1. 1–20 Luke 19. 28–40
	G			

3	Tu	**THOMAS THE APOSTLE****	Hab. 2. 1–4 Ps. 31. 1–6 Eph. 2. 19–end John 20. 24–29	*MP:* Ps. 92; 146 2 Sam. 15. 17–21 *or* Ecclus. ch. 2 John 11. 1–16
	R	*or, if Thomas is not celebrated:*	Amos 3. 1–8; 4. 11–12 Ps. 5. 8–end Matt. 8. 23–27	Ps. **106**† (*or* 103) 1 Sam. 1.21 – 2.11 Luke 19. 41–end
	G			

4	W		Amos 5. 14–15, 21–24 Ps. 50. 7–14 Matt. 8. 28–end	Ps, 110; **111**; 112 1 Sam. 2. 12–26 Luke 20. 1–8
	G			

5	Th		Amos 7. 10–end Ps. 19. 7–10 Matt. 9. 1–8	Ps. 113; **115** 1 Sam. 2. 27–end Luke 20. 9–19
	G			

6	F	*Thomas More, Scholar, and John Fisher, Bishop of Rochester, Reformation Martyrs, 1535*		
			Amos 8. 4–6, 9–12 Ps. 119. 1–8 Matt. 9. 9–13	Ps. 139 1 Sam. 3.1 – 4.1a Luke 20. 20–26
	G			

7	Sa	*****	Amos 9. 11–end Ps. 85. 8–end Matt. 9. 14–17	Ps. 120; **121**; 122 1 Sam. 4. 1b–end Luke 20. 27–40
	G			

8	S	**THE SIXTH SUNDAY AFTER TRINITY (Proper 9)**		
		Track 1 2 Sam. 5. 1–5, 9–10 Ps. 48 2 Cor. 12. 2–10 Mark 6. 1–13	*Track 2* Ezek. 2. 1–5 Ps. 123 2 Cor. 12. 2–10 Mark 6. 1–13	Ps. 57 Deut. 24. 10–end Acts 28. 1–16
	G			

*For Ember Day provision, see p. 11.
**The Visit of the Blessed Virgin Mary to Elizabeth may be celebrated on 2 July instead of 31 May.
***Common Worship Morning and Evening Prayer provision for 31 May may be used.
****Thomas the Apostle may be celebrated on 21 December instead of 3 July.
*****Thomas Becket may be celebrated on 7 July instead of 29 December.

Second Service Evening Prayer	Calendar and Holy Communion	Morning Prayer	Evening Prayer
Ps. 104 Neh. 9. 24–end Rom. 16. 17–end ct	G	Judg. 18. 1–20, 27–end Luke 19. 11–27	Neh. 9. 24–end Rom. 16. 17–end ct
	THE FIFTH SUNDAY AFTER TRINITY		
Ps. [52]; 53 Jer. 11. 1–14 Rom. 13. 1–10 Gospel: Luke 9. 51–end	1 Kings 19. 19–21 Ps. 84. 8–end 1 Pet. 3. 8–15a Luke 5. 1–11 G	Ps. 56 Deut. 15. 1–11 Acts 27. [13–32] 33–end	Ps. [52]; 53 Jer. 11. 1–14 Rom. 13. 1–10
Ps. *105*† (or 103) Neh. 12. 27–47 2 Cor. 1. 1–14 or First EP of Thomas Ps. 27 Isa. ch. 35 Heb. 10.35 – 11.1 R ct	**The Visitation of the Blessed Virgin Mary*** 1 Sam. 2. 1–3 Ps. 113 Gal. 4. 1–5 Luke 1. 39–45 Gw	1 Sam. 1. 1–20 Luke 19. 28–40	Neh. 12. 27–47 2 Cor. 1. 1–14
EP: Ps. 139 Job 42. 1–6 1 Pet. 1. 3–12	G	1 Sam. 1.21 – 2.11 Luke 19. 41–end	Neh. 13. 1–14 2 Cor. 1.15 – 2.4
Ps. 107† Neh. 13. 1–14 2 Cor. 1.15 – 2.4			
Ps. 119. 129–152 Neh. 13. 15–end 2 Cor. 2. 5–end	**Translation of Martin, Bishop of Tours, c. 397** Com. Bishop Gw	1 Sam. 2. 12–26 Luke 20. 1–8	Neh. 13. 15–end 2 Cor. 2. 5–end
Ps. 114; *116*; 117 Esther ch. 1 2 Cor. ch. 3	G	1 Sam. 2. 27–end Luke 20. 9–19	Esther ch. 1 2 Cor. ch. 3
Ps. *130*; 131; 137 Esther ch. 2 2 Cor. ch. 4	G	1 Sam. 3.1 – 4.1a Luke 20. 20–26	Esther ch. 2 2 Cor. ch. 4
Ps. 118 Esther ch. 3 2 Cor. ch. 5 ct	G	1 Sam. 4. 1b–end Luke 20. 27–40	Esther ch. 3 2 Cor. ch. 5 ct
	THE SIXTH SUNDAY AFTER TRINITY		
Ps. [63]; 64 Jer. 20. 1–11a Rom. 14. 1–17 Gospel: Luke 10. 1–11, 16–20	Gen. 4. 2b–15 Ps. 90. 12–end Rom. 6. 3–11 Matt. 5. 20–26 G	Ps. 57 Deut. 24. 10–end Acts 28. 1–16	Ps. [63]; 64 Jer. 20. 1–11a Rom. 14. 1–17

July 2018

		Sunday Principal Service / Weekday Eucharist	Third Service / Morning Prayer

9 M / DEL 14 G

		Sunday Principal Service Weekday Eucharist	Third Service Morning Prayer
9 DEL 14	M G	Hos. 2. 14–16, 19–20 Ps. 145. 2–9 Matt. 9. 18–26	Ps. 123; 124; 125; *126* I Sam. ch. 5 Luke 20.41 – 21.4
10	Tu G	Hos. 8. 4–7, 11–13 Ps. 103. 8–12 Matt. 9. 32–end	Ps. *132*; 133 I Sam. 6. 1–16 Luke 21. 5–19
11	W Gw	**Benedict of Nursia, Abbot of Monte Cassino, Father of Western Monasticism, c. 550** Com. Religious or Hos. 10. 1–3, 7–8, 12 *also* I Cor. 3. 10–11 Ps. 115. 3–10 Luke 18. 18–22 Matt. 10. 1–7	Ps. 119. 153–end I Sam. ch. 7 Luke 21. 20–28
12	Th G	Hos. 11. 1, 3–4, 8–9 Ps. 105. 1–7 Matt. 10. 7–15	Ps. *143*; 146 I Sam. ch. 8 Luke 21. 29–end
13	F G	Hos. 14. 2–end Ps. 80. 1–7 Matt. 10. 16–23	Ps. 142; *144* I Sam. 9. 1–14 Luke 22. 1–13
14	Sa Gw	**John Keble, Priest, Tractarian, Poet, 1866** Com. Pastor or Isa. 6. 1–8 *also* Lam. 3. 19–26 Ps. 51. 1–7 Matt. 5. 1–8 Matt. 10. 24–33	Ps. 147 I Sam. 9.15 – 10.1 Luke 22. 14–23
15	S G	THE SEVENTH SUNDAY AFTER TRINITY (**Proper 10**) *Track 1* *Track 2* 2 Sam. 6. 1–5, 12b–19 Amos 7. 7–15 Ps. 24 Ps. 85. 8–end Eph. 1. 3–14 Eph. 1. 3–14 Mark 6. 14–29 Mark 6. 14–29	Ps. 65 Deut. 28. 1–14 Acts 28. 17–end
16 DEL 15	M G	*Osmund, Bishop of Salisbury, 1099* Isa. 1. 11–17 Ps. 50. 7–15 Matt. 10.34 – 11.1	Ps. *1*; 2; 3 I Sam. 10. 1–16 Luke 22. 24–30
17	Tu G	Isa. 7. 1–9 Ps. 48. 1–7 Matt. 11. 20–24	Ps. *5*; 6; (8) I Sam. 10. 17–end Luke 22. 31–38
18	W G	*Elizabeth Ferard, first Deaconess of the Church of England, Founder of the Community of St Andrew, 1883* Isa. 10. 5–7, 13–16 Ps. 94. 5–11 Matt. 11. 25–27	Ps. 119. 1–32 I Sam. ch. 11 Luke 22. 39–46
19	Th Gw	**Gregory, Bishop of Nyssa, and his sister Macrina, Deaconess, Teachers, c. 394 and c. 379** Com. Teacher or Isa. 26. 7–9, 16–19 *esp.* I Cor. 2. 9–13 Ps. 102. 14–21 *also* Wisd. 9. 13–17 Matt. 11. 28–end	Ps. 14; *15*; 16 I Sam. ch. 12 Luke 22. 47–62
20	F G	*Margaret of Antioch, Martyr, 4th century; Bartolomé de las Casas, Apostle to the Indies, 1566* Isa. 38. 1–6, 21–22, 7–8 Canticle: Isa. 38. 10–16 *or* Ps. 32. 1–8 Matt. 12. 1–8	Ps. 17; *19* I Sam. 13. 5–18 Luke 22. 63–end
21	Sa G	Mic. 2. 1–5 Ps. 10. 1–5a, 12 Matt. 12. 14–21	Ps. 20; 21; *23* I Sam. 13.19 – 14.15 Luke 23. 1–12

G

Second Service Evening Prayer	Calendar and Holy Communion	Morning Prayer	Evening Prayer
Ps. *127*; 128; 129 Esther ch. 4 2 Cor. 6.1 – 7.1	G	I Sam. ch. 5 Luke 20.41 – 21.4	Esther ch. 4 2 Cor. 6.1 – 7.1
Ps. (134); *135* Esther ch. 5 2 Cor. 7. 2–end	G	I Sam. 6. 1–16 Luke 21. 5–19	Esther ch. 5 2 Cor. 7. 2–end
Ps. 136 Esther 6. 1–13 2 Cor. 8. 1–15	G	I Sam. ch. 7 Luke 21. 20–28	Esther 6. 1–13 2 Cor. 8. 1–15
Ps. *138*; 140; 141 Esther 6.14 – 7.end 2 Cor. 8.16 – 9.5	G	I Sam. ch. 8 Luke 21. 29–end	Esther 6.14 – 7.end 2 Cor. 8.16 – 9.5
Ps. 145 Esther ch. 8 2 Cor. 9. 6–end	G	I Sam. 9. 1–14 Luke 22. 1–13	Esther ch. 8 2 Cor. 9. 6–end
Ps. *148*; 149; 150 Esther 9. 20–28 2 Cor. ch. 10 ct	G	I Sam. 9.15 – 10.1 Luke 22. 14–23	Esther 9. 20–28 2 Cor. ch. 10 ct
	THE SEVENTH SUNDAY AFTER TRINITY		
Ps. 66 (or 66. 1–8) Job 4. 1; 5. 6–end or Ecclus. 4. 11–end Rom. 15. 14–29 *Gospel:* Luke 10. 25–37	I Kings 17. 8–16 Ps. 34. 11–end Rom. 6. 19–end Mark 8. 1–10a G	Ps. 65 Deut. 28. 1–14 Acts 28. 17–end	Ps. 66 (or 66. 1–8) Job 4. 1; 5. 6–end or Ecclus. 4. 11–end Luke 10. 21–24
Ps. *4*; 7 Jer. ch. 26 2 Cor. 11. 1–15	G	I Sam. 10. 1–16 Luke 22. 24–30	Jer. ch. 26 2 Cor. 11. 1–15
Ps. *9*; 10† Jer. ch. 28 2 Cor. 11. 16–end	G	I Sam. 10. 17–end Luke 22. 31–38	Jer. ch. 28 2 Cor. 11. 16–end
Ps. *11*; 12; 13 Jer. 29. 1–14 2 Cor. ch. 12	G	I Sam. ch. 11 Luke 22. 39–46	Jer. 29. 1–14 2 Cor. ch. 12
Ps. 18† Jer. 30. 1–11 2 Cor. ch. 13	G	I Sam. ch. 12 Luke 22. 47–62	Jer. 30. 1–11 2 Cor. ch. 13
Ps. 22 Jer. 30. 12–22 James 1. 1–11	**Margaret of Antioch, Martyr, 4th century** Com. Virgin Martyr Gr	I Sam. 13. 5–18 Luke 22. 63–end	Jer. 30. 12–22 James 1. 1–11
Ps. *24*; 25 Jer. 31. 1–22 James 1. 12–end ct or First EP of Mary Magdalene Ps. 139 Isa. 25. 1–9 2 Cor. 1. 3–7 **W** ct	G	I Sam. 13.19 – 14.15 Luke 23. 1–12	Jer. 31. 1–22 James 1. 12–end ct or First EP of Mary Magdalene (Ps. 139) Isa. 25. 1–9 2 Cor. 1. 3–7 **W** ct

July 2018

			Sunday Principal Service Weekday Eucharist	Third Service Morning Prayer

22	S	MARY MAGDALENE (or transferred to 23 July)	Song of Sol. 3. 1–4 Ps. 42. 1–10 2 Cor. 5. 14–17	MP: Ps. 30; 32; 150 1 Sam. 16. 14–end Luke 8. 1–3
	W		John 20. 1–2, 11–18	

or, for The Eighth Sunday after Trinity (Proper 11):

		Track 1	Track 2	
		2 Sam. 7. 1–14a Ps. 89. 20–37 Eph. 2. 11–end Mark 6. 30–34, 53–end	Jer. 23. 1–6 Ps. 23 Eph. 2. 11–end Mark 6. 30–34, 53–end	Ps. 67; 70 Deut. 30. 1–10 1 Pet. 3. 8–18
	G			

23 DEL 16	M	Bridget of Sweden, Abbess of Vadstena, 1373	Mic. 6. 1–4, 6–8 Ps. 50. 3–7, 14	Ps. 27; **30** 1 Sam. 14. 24–46
	G		Matt. 12. 38–42	Luke 23. 13–25
24	Tu		Mic. 7. 14–15, 18–20 Ps. 85. 1–7 Matt. 12. 46–end	Ps. 32; **36** 1 Sam. 15. 1–23 Luke 23. 26–43
	G			
25	W	JAMES THE APOSTLE	Jer. 45. 1–5 or Acts 11.27 – 12.2 Ps. 126 Acts 11.27 – 12.2 or 2 Cor. 4. 7–15	MP: Ps. 7; 29; 117 2 Kings 1. 9–15 Luke 9. 46–56
	R		Matt. 20. 20–28	
26	Th	**Anne and Joachim, Parents of the Blessed Virgin Mary** Zeph. 3. 14–18a or Ps. 127 Rom. 8. 28–30	Jer. 2. 1–3, 7–8, 12–13 Ps. 36. 5–10 Matt. 13. 10–17	Ps. 37† 1 Sam. 17. 1–30 Luke 23.56b – 24.12
	Gw		Matt. 13. 16–17	
27	F	Brooke Foss Westcott, Bishop of Durham, Teacher, 1901	Jer. 3. 14–17 Ps. 23 or Canticle: Jer. 31. 10–13	Ps. 31 1 Sam. 17. 31–54 Luke 24. 13–35
	G		Matt. 13. 18–23	
28	Sa		Jer. 7. 1–11 Ps. 84. 1–6 Matt. 13. 24–30	Ps. 41; **42**; 43 1 Sam. 17.55 – 18.16 Luke 24. 36–end
	G			
29	S	THE NINTH SUNDAY AFTER TRINITY **(Proper 12)** Track 1 2 Sam. 11. 1–15 Ps. 14 Eph. 3. 14–end John 6. 1–21	Track 2 2 Kings 4. 42–end Ps. 145. 10–19 Eph. 3. 14–end John 6. 1–21	Ps. 75 Song of Sol. ch. 2 or 1 Macc. 2. [1–14] 15–22 1 Pet. 4. 7–14
	G			
30 DEL 17	M	**William Wilberforce, Social Reformer, Olaudah Equiano and Thomas Clarkson, Anti-Slavery Campaigners, 1833, 1797 and 1846** Com. Saint or also Job 31. 16–23 Gal. 3. 26–end; 4. 6–7	Jer. 13. 1–11 Ps. 82 or Deut. 32. 18–21	Ps. 44 1 Sam. 19. 1–18 Acts 1. 1–14
	Gw		Luke 4. 16–21	Matt. 13. 31–35	
31	Tu	Ignatius of Loyola, Founder of the Society of Jesus, 1556	Jer. 14. 17–end Ps. 79. 8–end	Ps. **48**; 52 1 Sam. 20. 1–17
	G		Matt. 13. 36–43	Acts 1. 15–end

Second Service Evening Prayer		Calendar and Holy Communion	Morning Prayer	Evening Prayer
EP: Ps. 63 Zeph. 3. 14–end Mark 15.40 – 16.7	W	**MARY MAGDALENE** Zeph. 3. 14–end Ps. 30. 1–5 2 Cor. 5. 14–17 John 20. 11–18 *or, for The Eighth Sunday after Trinity:*	Ps. 30; 32; 150 I Sam. 16. 14–end Luke 8. 1–3	Ps. 63 Song of Sol. 3. 1–4 Mark 15.40 – 16.7
Ps. 73 (*or* 73. 21–end) Job 13.13 – 14.6 *or* Ecclus. 18. 1–14 Heb. 2. 5–end *Gospel:* Luke 10. 38–end	G	Jer. 23. 16–24 Ps. 31. 1–6 Rom. 8. 12–17 Matt. 7. 15–21	Ps. 67; 70 Deut. 30. 1–10 I Pet. 3. 13–22	Ps. 73 (*or* 73. 21–end) Job 13.13 – 14.6 *or* Ecclus. 18. 1–14 Heb. 2. 5–end
Ps. 26; *28*; 29 Jer. 31. 23–25, 27–37 James 2. 1–13	G		I Sam. 14. 24–46 Luke 23. 13–25	Jer. 31. 23–25, 27–37 James 2. 1–13
Ps. 33 Jer. 32. 1–15 James 2. 14–end *or First EP of James* Ps. 144 Deut. 30. 11–end Mark 5. 21–end **R ct**	G		I Sam. 15. 1–23 Luke 23. 26–43	Jer. 32. 1–15 James 2. 14–end *or First EP of James* (Ps. 144) Deut. 30. 11–end Mark 5. 21–end **R ct**
EP: Ps. 94 Jer. 26. 1–15 Mark 1. 14–20	R	**JAMES THE APOSTLE** 2 Kings 1. 9–15 Ps. 15 Acts 11.27 – 12.3a Matt. 20. 20–28	(Ps. 7; 29; 117) Jer. 45. 1–5 Luke 9. 46–56	(Ps. 94) Jer. 26. 1–15 Mark 1. 14–20
Ps. 39; *40* Jer. 33. 14–end James 4. 1–12	Gw	**Anne, Mother of the Blessed Virgin Mary** Com. Saint	I Sam. 17. 1–30 Luke 23.56b – 24.12	Jer. 33. 14–end James 4. 1–12
Ps. 35 Jer. ch. 35 James 4.13 – 5.6	G		I Sam. 17. 31–54 Luke 24. 13–35	Jer. ch. 35 James 4.13 – 5.6
Ps. 45; *46* Jer. 36. 1–18 James 5. 7–end ct	G		I Sam. 17.55 – 18.16 Luke 24. 36–end	Jer. 36. 1–18 James 5. 7–end ct
Ps. 74 (*or* 74. 11–16) Job 19. 1–27a *or* Ecclus. 38. 24–end Heb. ch. 8 *Gospel:* Luke 11. 1–13	G	**THE NINTH SUNDAY AFTER TRINITY** Num. 10.35 – 11.3 Ps. 95 I Cor. 10. 1–13 Luke 16. 1–9 *or* Luke 15. 11–end	Ps. 75 Song of Sol. ch. 2 *or* I Macc. 2. [1–14] 15–22 I Pet. 4. 7–14	Ps. 74 (*or* 74. 11–16) Job 19. 1–27a *or* Ecclus. 38. 24–end Heb. ch. 8
Ps. *47*; 49 Jer. 36. 19–end Mark 1. 1–13	G		I Sam. 19. 1–18 Acts 1. 1–14	Jer. 36. 19–end Mark 1. 1–13
Ps. 50 Jer. ch. 37 Mark 1. 14–20	G		I Sam. 20. 1–17 Acts 1. 15–end	Jer. ch. 37 Mark 1. 14–20

August 2018

			Sunday Principal Service Weekday Eucharist	Third Service Morning Prayer
1	W		Jer. 15. 10, 16–end Ps. 59. 1–4, 18–end	Ps. 119. 57–80 1 Sam. 20. 18–end
	G		Matt. 13. 44–46	Acts 2. 1–21
2	Th		Jer. 18. 1–6 Ps. 146. 1–5	Ps. 56; **57**; (63†) 1 Sam. 21.1 – 22.5
	G		Matt. 13. 47–53	Acts 2. 22–36
3	F		Jer. 26. 1–9 Ps. 69. 4–10	Ps. **51**; 54 1 Sam. 22. 6–end
	G		Matt. 13. 54–end	Acts 2. 37–end
4	Sa	Jean-Baptiste Vianney, Curé d'Ars, Spiritual Guide, 1859		
			Jer. 26. 11–16, 24 Ps. 69. 14–20	Ps. 68
	G		Matt. 14. 1–12	1 Sam. ch. 23 Acts 3. 1–10
5	S	THE TENTH SUNDAY AFTER TRINITY **(Proper 13)** Track 1 2 Sam. 11.26 – 12.13a Ps. 51. 1–13 Eph. 4. 1–16 John 6. 24–35	Track 2 Exod. 16. 2–4, 9–15 Ps. 78. 23–29 Eph. 4. 1–16 John 6. 24–35	Ps. 86 Song of Sol. 5. 2–end or 1 Macc. 3. 1–12 2 Pet. 1. 1–15
	G			
6 DEL 18	M	THE TRANSFIGURATION OF OUR LORD	Dan. 7. 9–10, 13–14 Ps. 97 2 Pet. 1. 16–19	MP: Ps. 27; 150 Ecclus. 48. 1–10 or 1 Kings 19. 1–16
	𝍫		Luke 9. 28–36	1 John 3. 1–3
7	Tu	John Mason Neale, Priest, Hymn Writer, 1866	Jer. 30. 1–2, 12–15, 18–22 Ps. 102. 16–21 Matt. 14. 22–end or 15. 1–2,	Ps. 73 1 Sam. ch. 26 Acts 4. 1–12
	G		10–14	
8	W	**Dominic, Priest, Founder of the Order of Preachers, 1221** Com. Religious or also Ecclus. 39. 1–10	Jer. 31. 1–7 Ps. 121	Ps. 77 1 Sam. 28. 3–end
	Gw		Matt. 15. 21–28	Acts 4. 13–31
9	Th	**Mary Sumner, Founder of the Mothers' Union, 1921** Com. Saint or also Heb. 13. 1–5	Jer. 31. 31–34 Ps. 51. 11–18	Ps. 78. 1–39† 1 Sam. ch. 31
	Gw		Matt. 16. 13–23	Acts 4.32 – 5.11
10	F	**Laurence, Deacon at Rome, Martyr, 258** Com. Martyr or also 2 Cor. 9. 6–10	Nahum 2. 1, 3; 3. 1–3, 6–7 Ps. 137. 1–6 or Deut. 32. 35–36, 39, 41	Ps. 55 2 Sam. ch. 1 Acts 5. 12–26
	Gr		Matt. 16. 24–28	
11	Sa	**Clare of Assisi, Founder of the Minoresses (Poor Clares), 1253** John Henry Newman, Priest, Tractarian, 1890 Com. Religious or esp. Song of Sol. 8. 6–7	Hab. 1.12 – 2.4 Ps. 9. 7–11 Matt. 17. 14–20	Ps. **76**; 79 2 Sam. 2. 1–11 Acts 5. 27–end
	Gw			
12	S	THE ELEVENTH SUNDAY AFTER TRINITY **(Proper 14)** Track 1 2 Sam. 18. 5–9, 15, 31–33 Ps. 130 Eph. 4.25 – 5.2 John 6. 35, 41–51	Track 2 1 Kings 19. 4–8 Ps. 34. 1–8 Eph. 4.25 – 5.2 John 6. 35, 41–51	Ps. 90 Song of Sol. 8. 5–7 or 1 Macc. 14. 4–15 2 Pet. 3. 8–13
	G			

Second Service Evening Prayer	Calendar and Holy Communion	Morning Prayer	Evening Prayer
Ps. *59*; 60; (67) Jer. 38. 1–13 Mark 1. 21–28	Lammas Day G	1 Sam. 20. 18–end Acts 2. 1–21	Jer. 38. 1–13 Mark 1. 21–28
Ps. 61; *62*; 64 Jer. 38. 14–end Mark 1. 29–end	 G	1 Sam. 21.1 – 22.5 Acts 2. 22–36	Jer. 38. 14–end Mark 1. 29–end
Ps. 38 Jer. ch. 39 Mark 2. 1–12	 G	1 Sam. 22. 6–end Acts 2. 37–end	Jer. ch. 39 Mark 2. 1–12
Ps. 65; *66* Jer. ch. 40 Mark 2. 13–22 ct	 G	1 Sam. ch. 23 Acts 3. 1–10	Jer. ch. 40 Mark 2. 13–22 ct
	THE TENTH SUNDAY AFTER TRINITY		
Ps. 88 (or 88. 1–10) Job ch. 28 or Ecclus. 42. 15–end Heb. 11. 17–31 *Gospel: Luke 12. 13–21* *or First EP of The* *Transfiguration* Ps. 99; 110 Exod. 24. 12–end John 12. 27–36a ℣ ct	Jer. 7. 9–15 Ps. 17. 1–8 1 Cor. 12. 1–11 Luke 19. 41–47a G	Ps. 86 Song of Sol. 5. 2–end or 1 Macc. 3. 1–12 2 Pet. 1. 1–15	Ps. 88 (or 88. 1–10) Job ch. 28 or Ecclus. 42. 15–end Heb. 11. 17–31 *or First EP of The* *Transfiguration* Ps. 99; 110 Exod. 24. 12–end John 12. 27–36a ℣ ct
	THE TRANSFIGURATION OF OUR LORD		
EP: Ps. 72 Exod. 34. 29–end 2 Cor. ch. 3	Exod. 24. 12–end Ps. 84. 1–7 1 John 3. 1–3 ℣ Mark 9. 2–7	(Ps. 27; 150) Ecclus. 48. 1–10 or 1 Kings 19. 1–16 2 Pet. 1. 16–19	(Ps. 72) Exod. 34. 29–end 2 Cor. ch. 3
	The Name of Jesus		
Ps. 74 Jer. ch. 42 Mark 3. 7–19a	Jer. 14. 7–9 Ps. 8 Acts 4. 8–12 Gw Matt. 1. 20–23	1 Sam. ch. 26 Acts 4. 1–12	Jer. ch. 42 Mark 3. 7–19a
Ps. 119. 81–104 Jer. ch. 43 Mark 3. 19b–end	 G	1 Sam. 28. 3–end Acts 4. 13–31	Jer. ch. 43 Mark 3. 19b–end
Ps. 78. 40–end† Jer. 44. 1–14 Mark 4. 1–20	 G	1 Sam. ch. 31 Acts 4.32 – 5.11	Jer. 44. 1–14 Mark 4. 1–20
	Laurence, Deacon at Rome, Martyr, 258		
Ps. 69 Jer. 44. 15–end Mark 4. 21–34	Com. Martyr Gr	2 Sam. ch. 1 Acts 5. 12–26	Jer. 44. 15–end Mark 4. 21–34
Ps. *81*; 84 Jer. ch. 45 Mark 4. 35–end ct	 G	2 Sam. 2. 1–11 Acts 5. 27–end	Jer. ch. 45 Mark 4. 35–end ct
	THE ELEVENTH SUNDAY AFTER TRINITY		
Ps. 91 (or 91. 1–12) Job 39.1 – 40.4 or Ecclus. 43. 13–end Heb. 12. 1–17 *Gospel: Luke 12. 32–40*	1 Kings 3. 5–15 Ps. 28 1 Cor. 15. 1–11 Luke 18. 9–14 G	Ps. 89. 1–18 Song of Sol. 8. 5–7 or 1 Macc. 14. 4–15 2 Pet. 3. 8–13	Ps. 91 (or 91. 1–12) Job 39.1 – 40.4 or Ecclus. 43. 13–end Heb. 12. 1–17

August 2018

		Sunday Principal Service / Weekday Eucharist		Third Service / Morning Prayer

13 DEL 19

M **Jeremy Taylor, Bishop of Down and Connor, Teacher, 1667**
Florence Nightingale, Nurse, Social Reformer, 1910; Octavia Hill, Social Reformer, 1912

	Com. Teacher	*or*	Ezek. 1. 2–5, 24–end	Ps. *80*; 82
	also Titus 2. 7–8, 11–14		Ps. 148. 1–4, 12–13	2 Sam. 3. 12–end
Gw			Matt. 17. 22–end	Acts ch. 6

14

Tu *Maximilian Kolbe, Friar, Martyr, 1941*

	Ezek. 2.8 – 3.4	Ps. 87; *89. 1–18*
	Ps. 119. 65–72	2 Sam. 5. 1–12
	Matt. 18. 1–5, 10, 12–14	Acts 7. 1–16

G

15

W THE BLESSED VIRGIN MARY*

	Isa. 61. 10–end	MP: Ps. 98; 138; 147. 1–12
	or Rev. 11.19 – 12.6, 10	Isa. 7. 10–15
	Ps. 45. 10–end	Luke 11. 27–28
	Gal. 4. 4–7	
W	Luke 1. 46–55	

or, if The Blessed Virgin Mary is celebrated on 8 September:

	Ezek. 9. 1–7; 10. 18–22	Ps. 119. 105–128
	Ps. 113	2 Sam. 6. 1–19
G	Matt. 18. 15–20	Acts 7. 17–43

16

Th	Ezek. 12. 1–12	Ps. 90; *92*
	Ps. 78. 58–64	2 Sam. 7. 1–17
G	Matt. 18.21 – 19.1	Acts 7. 44–53

17

F	Ezek. 16. 1–15, 60–end	Ps. *88*; (95)
	Ps. 118. 14–18	2 Sam. 7. 18–end
	or Canticle: Song of Deliverance	Acts 7.54 – 8.3
G	Matt. 19. 3–12	

18

Sa	Ezek. 18. 1–11a, 13b, 30, 32	Ps. 96; *97*; 100
	Ps. 51. 1–3, 15–17	2 Sam. ch. 9
	Matt. 19. 13–15	Acts 8. 4–25
G		

19

S THE TWELFTH SUNDAY AFTER TRINITY **(Proper 15)**

Track 1	*Track 2*	
1 Kings 2. 10–12; 3. 3–14	Prov. 9. 1–6	Ps. 106. 1–10
Ps. 111	Ps. 34. 9–14	Jonah ch. 1
Eph. 5. 15–20	Eph. 5. 15–20	*or* Ecclus. 3. 1–15
G John 6. 51–58	John 6. 51–58	2 Pet. 3. 14–end

20 DEL 20

M **Bernard, Abbot of Clairvaux, Teacher, 1153**
William and Catherine Booth, Founders of the Salvation Army, 1912 and 1890

	Com. Teacher	*or*	Ezek. 24. 15–24	Ps. *98*; 99; 101
	esp. Rev. 19. 5–9		Ps. 78. 1–8	2 Sam. ch. 11
Gw			Matt. 19. 16–22	Acts 8. 26–end

21

Tu	Ezek. 28. 1–10	Ps. *106*† (*or* 103)
	Ps. 107. 1–3, 40, 43	2 Sam. 12. 1–25
G	Matt. 19. 23–end	Acts 9. 1–19a

22

W	Ezek. 34. 1–11	Ps. 110; *111*; 112
	Ps. 23	2 Sam. 15. 1–12
G	Matt. 20. 1–16	Acts 9. 19b–31

23

Th	Ezek. 36. 23–28	Ps. 113; *115*
	Ps. 51. 7–12	2 Sam. 15. 13–end
	Matt. 22. 1–14	Acts 9. 32–end

G

*The Blessed Virgin Mary may be celebrated on 8 September instead of 15 August.

Second Service Evening Prayer	Calendar and Holy Communion	Morning Prayer	Evening Prayer
Ps. *85*; 86 Mic. 1. 1–9 Mark 5. 1–20	G	2 Sam. 3. 12–end Acts ch. 6	Mic. 1. 1–9 Mark 5. 1–20
Ps. 89. 19–end Mic. ch. 2 Mark 5. 21–34 or First EP of The Blessed Virgin Mary Ps. 72 Prov. 8. 22–31 John 19. 23–27 **W ct**	G	2 Sam. 5. 1–12 Acts 7. 1–16	Mic. ch. 2 Mark 5. 21–34
EP: Ps. 132 Song of Sol. 2. 1–7 Acts 1. 6–14	To celebrate The Blessed Virgin Mary, see *Common Worship* provision. 2 Sam. 6. 1–19 Acts 7. 17–43	Mic. ch. 3 Mark 5. 35–end
Ps. *91*; 93 Mic. ch. 3 Mark 5. 35–end	G		
Ps. 94 Mic. 4.1 – 5.1 Mark 6. 1–13	G	2 Sam. 7. 1–17 Acts 7. 44–53	Mic. 4.1 – 5.1 Mark 6. 1–13
Ps. 102 Mic. 5. 2–end Mark 6. 14–29	G	2 Sam. 7. 18–end Acts 7.54 – 8.3	Mic. 5. 2–end Mark 6. 14–29
Ps. 104 Mic. ch. 6 Mark 6. 30–44 ct	G	2 Sam. ch. 9 Acts 8. 4–25	Mic. ch. 6 Mark 6. 30–44 ct
	THE TWELFTH SUNDAY AFTER TRINITY		
Ps. [92]; 100 Exod. 2.23 – 3.10 Heb. 13. 1–15 *Gospel:* Luke 12. 49–56	Exod. 34. 29–end Ps. 34. 1–10 2 Cor. 3. 4–9 Mark 7. 31–37 G	Ps. 106. 1–10 Jonah ch. 1 or Ecclus. 3. 1–15 2 Pet. 3. 14–end	Ps. [92]; 100 Exod. 2.23 – 3.10 Heb. 13. 1–15
Ps. *105*† (or 103) Mic. 7. 1–7 Mark 6. 45–end	G	2 Sam. ch. 11 Acts 8. 26–end	Mic. 7. 1–7 Mark 6. 45–end
Ps. 107† Mic. 7. 8–end Mark 7. 1–13	G	2 Sam. 12. 1–25 Acts 9. 1–19a	Mic. 7. 8–end Mark 7. 1–13
Ps. 119. 129–152 Hab. 1. 1–11 Mark 7. 14–23	G	2 Sam. 15. 1–12 Acts 9. 19b–31	Hab. 1. 1–11 Mark 7. 14–23
Ps. 114; *116*; 117 Hab. 1.12 – 2.5 Mark 7. 24–30 or First EP of Bartholomew Ps. 97 Isa. 61. 1–9 2 Cor. 6. 1–10 **R ct**	G	2 Sam. 15. 13–end Acts 9. 32–end	Hab. 1.12 – 2.5 Mark 7. 24–30 or First EP of Bartholomew (Ps. 97) Isa. 61. 1–9 2 Cor. 6. 1–10 **R ct**

August 2018

			Sunday Principal Service / Weekday Eucharist	Third Service / Morning Prayer

			Sunday Principal Service **Weekday Eucharist**	**Third Service** **Morning Prayer**
24	F	BARTHOLOMEW THE APOSTLE	Isa. 43. 8–13 *or* Acts 5. 12–16 Ps. 145. 1–7 Acts 5. 12–16 *or* 1 Cor. 4. 9–15	*MP*: Ps. 86; 117 Gen. 28. 10–17 John 1. 43–end
	R		Luke 22. 24–30	
25	Sa		Ezek. 43. 1–7 Ps. 85. 7–end Matt. 23. 1–12	Ps. 120; *121*; 122 2 Sam. 17. 1–23 Acts 10. 17–33
	G			
26	S	THE THIRTEENTH SUNDAY AFTER TRINITY **(Proper 16)** *Track 1* 1 Kings 8. [1, 6, 10–11] 22–30, 41–43 Ps. 84 Eph. 6. 10–20	*Track 2* Josh. 24. 1–2a, 14–18 Ps. 34. 15–end Eph. 6. 10–20 John 6. 56–69	Ps. 115 Jonah ch. 2 *or* Ecclus. 3. 17–29 Rev. ch. 1
	G	John 6. 56–69		
27 DEL 21	M	**Monica, Mother of Augustine of Hippo, 387** Com. Saint *also* Ecclus. 26. 1–3, 13–16	*or* 2 Thess. 1. 1–5, 11–end Ps. 39. 1–9	Ps. 123; 124; 125; *126* 2 Sam. 18. 1–18
	Gw		Matt. 23. 13–22	Acts 10. 34–end
28	Tu	**Augustine, Bishop of Hippo, Teacher, 430** Com. Teacher *esp.* Ecclus. 39. 1–10	*or* 2 Thess. 2. 1–3a, 14–end Ps. 98	Ps. *132*; 133 2 Sam. 18.19 – 19.8a
	Gw	*also* Rom. 13. 11–13	Matt. 23. 23–26	Acts 11. 1–18
29	W	**The Beheading of John the Baptist** Jer. 1. 4–10 Ps. 11 Heb. 11.32 – 12.2	*or* 2 Thess. 3. 6–10, 16–end Ps. 128	Ps. 119. 153–end 2 Sam. 19. 8b–23
	Gr	Matt. 14. 1–12	Matt. 23. 27–32	Acts 11. 19–end
30	Th	**John Bunyan, Spiritual Writer, 1688** Com. Teacher *also* Heb. 12. 1–2	*or* 1 Cor. 1. 1–9 Ps. 145. 1–2	Ps. *143*; 146 2 Sam. 19. 24–end
	Gw	Luke 21. 21, 34–36	Matt. 24. 42–end	Acts 12. 1–17
31	F	**Aidan, Bishop of Lindisfarne, Missionary, 651** Com. Missionary *also* 1 Cor. 9. 16–19	*or* 1 Cor. 1. 17–25 Ps. 33. 6–12	Ps. 142; *144* 2 Sam. 23. 1–7
	Gw		Matt. 25. 1–13	Acts 12. 18–end

September 2018

1	Sa	*Giles of Provence, Hermit, c. 710*	1 Cor. 1. 26–end Ps. 33. 12–15, 20–end Matt. 25. 14–30	Ps. 147 2 Sam. ch. 24 Acts 13. 1–12
	G			
2	S	THE FOURTEENTH SUNDAY AFTER TRINITY **(Proper 17)** *Track 1* Song of Sol. 2. 8–13 Ps. 45. 1–2, 6–9 (*or* 1–7) James 1. 17–end Mark 7. 1–8, 14–15, 21–23	*Track 2* Deut. 4. 1–2, 6–9 Ps. 15 James 1. 17–end Mark 7. 1–8, 14–15, 21–23	Ps. 119. 17–40 Jonah 3. 1–9 *or* Ecclus. 11. 7–28 (*or* 19–28) Rev. 3. 14–end
	G			
3	M	**Gregory the Great, Bishop of Rome, Teacher, 604** Com. Teacher *also* 1 Thess. 2. 3–8	*or* 1 Cor. 2. 1–5 Ps. 33. 12–21	Ps. *1*; 2; 3 1 Kings 1. 5–31
DEL 22	Gw		Luke 4. 16–30	Acts 13. 13–43

Second Service Evening Prayer		Calendar and Holy Communion	Morning Prayer	Evening Prayer
EP: Ps. 91; 116 Ecclus. 39. 1–10 or Deut. 18. 15–19 Matt. 10. 1–22	R	**BARTHOLOMEW THE APOSTLE** Gen. 28. 10–17 Ps. 15 Acts 5. 12–16 Luke 22. 24–30	(Ps. 86; 117) Isa. 43. 8–13 John 1. 43–end	(Ps. 91; 116) Ecclus. 39. 1–10 or Deut. 18. 15–19 Matt. 10. 1–22
Ps. 118 Hab. 3. 2–19a Mark 8. 1–10 ct	G		2 Sam. 17. 1–23 Acts 10. 17–33	Hab. 3. 2–19a Mark 8. 1–10 ct
Ps. 116 (or 116. 10–end) Exod. 4.27 – 5.1 Heb. 13. 16–21 *Gospel*: Luke 13. 10–17	G	**THE THIRTEENTH SUNDAY AFTER TRINITY** Lev. 19. 13–18 Ps. 74. 20–end Gal. 3. 16–22 or Heb. 13. 1–6 Luke 10. 23b–37	Ps. 115 Jonah ch. 2 or Ecclus. 3. 17–29 Rev. ch. 1	Ps. 116 (or 116. 10–end) Exod. 4.27 – 5.1 Heb. 13. 16–21
Ps. *127*; 128; 129 Hag. 1. 1–11 Mark 8. 11–21	G		2 Sam. 18. 1–18 Acts 10. 34–end	Hag. 1. 1–11 Mark 8. 11–21
Ps. (134); *135* Hag. 1.12 – 2.9 Mark 8. 22–26	Gw	**Augustine, Bishop of Hippo, Teacher, 430** Com. Doctor	2 Sam. 18.19 – 19.8a Acts 11. 1–18	Hag. 1.12 – 2.9 Mark 8. 22–26
Ps. 136 Hag. 2. 10–end Mark 8.27 – 9.1	Gr	**The Beheading of John the Baptist** 2 Chron. 24. 17–21 Ps. 92. 11–end Heb. 11.32 – 12.2 Matt. 14. 1–12	2 Sam. 19. 8b–23 Acts 11. 19–end	Hag. 2. 10–end Mark 8.27 – 9.1
Ps. *138*; 140; 141 Zech. 1. 1–17 Mark 9. 2–13	G		2 Sam. 19. 24–end Acts 12. 1–17	Zech. 1. 1–17 Mark 9. 2–13
Ps. 145 Zech. 1.18 – 2.end Mark 9. 14–29	G		2 Sam. 23. 1–7 Acts 12. 18–end	Zech. 1.18 – 2.end Mark 9. 14–29
Ps. *148*; 149; 150 Zech. ch. 3 Mark 9. 30–37 ct	Gw	**Giles of Provence, Hermit, c. 710** Com. Abbot	2 Sam. ch. 24 Acts 13. 1–12	Zech. ch. 3 Mark 9. 30–37 ct
Ps. 119. 1–16 (or 9–16) Exod. 12. 21–27 Matt. 4.23 – 5.20	G	**THE FOURTEENTH SUNDAY AFTER TRINITY** 2 Kings 5. 9–16 Ps. 118. 1–9 Gal. 5. 16–24 Luke 17. 11–19	Ps. 119. 17–40 Jonah 3. 1–9 or Ecclus. 11. 7–28 (or 19–28) Rev. 3. 14–end	Ps. 119. 1–16 (or 9–16) Exod. 12. 21–27 Matt. 4.23 – 5.20
Ps. *4*; 7 Zech. ch. 4 Mark 9. 38–end	G		1 Kings 1. 5–31 Acts 13. 13–43	Zech. ch. 4 Mark 9. 38–end

September 2018

			Sunday Principal Service Weekday Eucharist	Third Service Morning Prayer
4	Tu	Birinus, Bishop of Dorchester (Oxon), Apostle of Wessex, 650*	I Cor. 2. 10b–end Ps. 145. 10–17	Ps. **5**; 6; (8) I Kings 1.32 – 2.4, 10–12
	G		Luke 4. 31–37	Acts 13.44 – 14.7
5	W		I Cor. 3. 1–9 Ps. 62	Ps. 119. 1–32 I Kings ch. 3
	G		Luke 4. 38–end	Acts 14. 8–end
6	Th	Allen Gardiner, Founder of the South American Mission Society, 1851	I Cor. 3. 18–end Ps. 24. 1–6	Ps. 14; **15**; 16 I Kings 4.29 – 5.12
	G		Luke 5. 1–11	Acts 15. 1–21
7	F		I Cor. 4. 1–5 Ps. 37. 3–8	Ps. 17; **19** I Kings 6. 1, 11–28
	G		Luke 5. 33–end	Acts 15. 22–35
8	Sa	**The Birth of the Blessed Virgin Mary**** Com. BVM or	I Cor. 4. 6–15 Ps. 145. 18–end Luke 6. 1–5	Ps. 20; 21; **23** I Kings 8. 1–30 Acts 15.36 – 16.5
	Gw			
9	S	THE FIFTEENTH SUNDAY AFTER TRINITY **(Proper 18)** Track 1 Prov. 22. 1–2, 8–9, 22–23 Ps. 125 James 2. 1–10 [11–13] 14–17	Track 2 Isa. 35. 4–7a Ps. 146 James 2. 1–10 [11–13] 14–17	Ps. 119. 57–72 Jonah 3.10 – 4.11 or Ecclus. 27.30 – 28.9
	G	Mark 7. 24–end	Mark 7. 24–end	Rev. 8. 1–5
10 DEL 23	M		I Cor. 5. 1–8 Ps. 5. 5–9a	Ps. 27; **30** I Kings 8. 31–62
	G		Luke 6. 6–11	Acts 16. 6–24
11	Tu		I Cor. 6. 1–11 Ps. 149. 1–5	Ps. 32; **36** I Kings 8.63 – 9.9
	G		Luke 6. 12–19	Acts 16. 25–end
12	W		I Cor. 7. 25–31 Ps. 45. 11–end	Ps. 34 I Kings 10. 1–25
	G		Luke 6. 20–26	Acts 17. 1–15
13	Th	**John Chrysostom, Bishop of Constantinople, Teacher, 407** Com. Teacher or esp. Matt. 5. 13–19 also Jer. 1. 4–10	I Cor. 8. 1–7, 11–end Ps. 139. 1–9 Luke 6. 27–38	Ps. 37† I Kings 11. 1–13 Acts 17. 16–end
	Gw			
14	F	HOLY CROSS DAY	Num. 21. 4–9 Ps. 22. 23–28 Phil. 2. 6–11	MP: Ps. 2; 8; 146 Gen. 3. 1–15 John 12. 27–36a
	R		John 3. 13–17	
15	Sa	**Cyprian, Bishop of Carthage, Martyr, 258** Com. Martyr or esp. I Pet. 4. 12–end also Matt. 18. 18–22	I Cor. 10. 14–22 Ps. 116. 10–end Luke 6. 43–end	Ps. 41; **42**; 43 I Kings 12. 1–24 Acts 18.22 – 19.7
	Gr			

*Cuthbert may be celebrated on 4 September instead of 20 March.
**The Blessed Virgin Mary may be celebrated on 8 September instead of 15 August.

Second Service Evening Prayer	Calendar and Holy Communion	Morning Prayer	Evening Prayer
Ps. **9**; 10† Zech. 6. 9–end Mark 10. 1–16	G	I Kings 1.32 – 2.4, 10–12 Acts 13.44 – 14.7	Zech. 6. 9–end Mark 10. 1–16
Ps. *11*; 12; 13 Zech. ch. 7 Mark 10. 17–31	G	I Kings ch. 3 Acts 14. 8–end	Zech. ch. 7 Mark 10. 17–31
Ps. 18† Zech. 8. 1–8 Mark 10. 32–34	G	I Kings 4.29 – 5.12 Acts 15. 1–21	Zech. 8. 1–8 Mark 10. 32–34
Ps. 22 Zech. 8. 9–end Mark 10. 35–45	**Evurtius, Bishop of Orleans, 4th century** Com. Bishop I Kings 6. 1, 11–28 Acts 15. 22–35 Gw	Zech. 8. 9–end Mark 10. 35–45
Ps. **24**; 25 Zech. 9. 1–12 Mark 10. 46–end ct	**The Birth of the Blessed Virgin Mary** Gen. 3. 9–15 I Kings 8. 1–30 Ps. 45. 11–18 Acts 15.36 – 16.5 Rom. 5. 12–17 Luke 11. 27–28 Gw	Zech. 9. 1–12 Mark 10. 46–end ct
Ps. 119. 41–56 (or 49–56) Exod. 14. 5–end Matt. 6. 1–18	THE FIFTEENTH SUNDAY AFTER TRINITY Josh. 24. 14–25 Ps. 119. 57–72 Ps. 92. 1–6 Jonah 3.10 – 4.11 Gal. 6. 11–end or Ecclus. 27.30 – 28.9 Matt. 6. 24–end Rev. 8. 1–5 G	Ps. 119. 41–56 (or 49–56) Exod. 14. 5–end Matt. 6. 1–18
Ps. 26; **28**; 29 Zech. ch. 10 Mark 11. 1–11	G	I Kings 8. 31–62 Acts 16. 6–24	Zech. ch. 10 Mark 11. 1–11
Ps. 33 Zech. 11. 4–end Mark 11. 12–26	G	I Kings 8.63 – 9.9 Acts 16. 25–end	Zech. 11. 4–end Mark 11. 12–26
Ps. 119. 33–56 Zech. 12. 1–10 Mark 11. 27–end	G	I Kings 10. 1–25 Acts 17. 1–15	Zech. 12. 1–10 Mark 11. 27–end
Ps. 39; **40** Zech. ch. 13 Mark 12. 1–12 or First EP of Holy Cross Day Ps. 66 Isa. 52.13 – 53.end Eph. 2. 11–end **R** ct	G	I Kings 11. 1–13 Acts 17. 16–end	Zech. ch. 13 Mark 12. 1–12
EP: Ps. 110; 150 Isa. 63. 1–16 I Cor. 1. 18–25	**Holy Cross Day** To celebrate Holy Cross as a festival, see *Common Worship* provision. Num. 21. 4–9 I Kings 11. 26–end Ps. 67 Acts 18. 1–21 I Cor. 1. 17–25 John 12. 27–33 Gr	Zech. 14. 1–11 Mark 12. 13–17
Ps. 45; **46** Zech. 14. 12–end Mark 12. 18–27 ct	G	I Kings 12. 1–24 Acts 18.22 – 19.7	Zech. 14. 12–end Mark 12. 18–27 ct

September 2018

		Sunday Principal Service Weekday Eucharist	Third Service Morning Prayer

16 S — THE SIXTEENTH SUNDAY AFTER TRINITY (Proper 19)

		Sunday Principal Service Weekday Eucharist	Third Service Morning Prayer
16 S	Track 1 Prov. 1. 20–33 Ps. 19 (or 19. 1–6) or Canticle: Wisd. 7.26 – 8.1 James 3. 1–12	Track 2 Isa. 50. 4–9a Ps. 116. 1–8 James 3. 1–12 Mark 8. 27–end	Ps. 119. 105–120 Isa. 44.24 – 45.8 Rev. 12. 1–12
G	Mark 8. 27–end		
17 M DEL 24	**Hildegard, Abbess of Bingen, Visionary, 1179** Com. Religious also 1 Cor. 2. 9–13 Luke 10. 21–24	or	1 Cor. 11. 17–26, 33 Ps. 40. 7–11 Luke 7. 1–10	Ps. 44 1 Kings 12.25 – 13.10 Acts 19. 8–20
Gw			
18 Tu		1 Cor. 12. 12–14, 27–end Ps. 100 Luke 7. 11–17	Ps. **48**; 52 1 Kings 13. 11–end Acts 19. 21–end
G			
19 W	Theodore of Tarsus, Archbishop of Canterbury, 690		
		1 Cor. 12.13b – 13.end Ps. 33. 1–12 Luke 7. 31–35	Ps. 119. 57–80 1 Kings ch. 17 Acts 20. 1–16
G			
20 Th	**John Coleridge Patteson, first Bishop of Melanesia, and his Companions, Martyrs, 1871** Com. Martyr esp. 2 Chron. 24. 17–21 also Acts 7. 55–end	or	1 Cor. 15. 1–11 Ps. 118. 1–2, 17–20 Luke 7. 36–end	Ps. 56; **57**; (63†) 1 Kings 18. 1–20 Acts 20. 17–end
Gr			
21 F	MATTHEW, APOSTLE AND EVANGELIST		
		Prov. 3. 13–18 Ps. 119. 65–72 2 Cor. 4. 1–6 Matt. 9. 9–13	MP: Ps. 49; 117 1 Kings 19. 15–end 2 Tim. 3. 14–end
R			
22 Sa		1 Cor. 15. 35–37, 42–49 Ps. 30. 1–5 Luke 8. 4–15	Ps. 68 1 Kings ch. 19 Acts 21. 17–36
G			
23 S	THE SEVENTEENTH SUNDAY AFTER TRINITY (Proper 20) Track 1 Prov. 31. 10–end Ps. 1 James 3.13 – 4.3, 7–8a Mark 9. 30–37	Track 2 Wisd. 1.16 – 2.1, 12–22 or Jer. 11. 18–20 Ps. 54 James 3.13 – 4.3, 7–8a Mark 9. 30–37	Ps. 119. 153–end Isa. 45. 9–22 Rev. 14. 1–5
G			
24 M DEL 25		Prov. 3. 27–34 Ps. 15 Luke 8. 16–18	Ps. 71 1 Kings ch. 21 Acts 21.37 – 22.21
G			
25 Tu	**Lancelot Andrewes, Bishop of Winchester, Spiritual Writer, 1626** Sergei of Radonezh, Russian Monastic Reformer, Teacher, 1392 Com. Bishop esp. Isa. 6. 1–8	or	Prov. 21. 1–6, 10–13 Ps. 119. 1–8 Luke 8. 19–21	Ps. 73 1 Kings 22. 1–28 Acts 22.22 – 23.11
Gw			

Second Service Evening Prayer	Calendar and Holy Communion		Morning Prayer	Evening Prayer
	THE SIXTEENTH SUNDAY AFTER TRINITY			
Ps. 119. 73–88 (or 73–80) Exod. 18. 13–26 Matt. 7. 1–14	1 Kings 17. 17–end Ps. 102. 12–17 Eph. 3. 13–end Luke 7. 11–17	G	Ps. 119. 105–120 Isa. 44.24 – 45.8 Rev. 12. 1–12	Ps. 119. 73–88 (or 73–80) Exod. 18. 13–26 Matt. 7. 1–14
Ps. 47; 49 Ecclus. 1. 1–10 or Ezek. 1. 1–14 Mark 12. 28–34	**Lambert, Bishop of Maastricht, Martyr, 709** Com. Martyr	Gr	1 Kings 12.25 – 13.10 Acts 19. 8–20	Ecclus. 1. 1–10 or Ezek. 1. 1–14 Mark 12. 28–34
Ps. 50 Ecclus. 1. 11–end or Ezek. 1.15 – 2.2 Mark 12. 35–end		G	1 Kings 13. 11–end Acts 19. 21–end	Ecclus. 1. 11–end or Ezek. 1.15 – 2.2 Mark 12. 35–end
Ps. 59; 60; (67) Ecclus. ch. 2 or Ezek. 2.3 – 3.11 Mark 13. 1–13	Ember Day Ember CEG	G	1 Kings ch. 17 Acts 20. 1–16	Ecclus. ch. 2 or Ezek. 2.3 – 3.11 Mark 13. 1–13
Ps. 61; 62; 64 Ecclus. 3. 17–29 or Ezek. 3. 12–end Mark 13. 14–23 or First EP of Matthew Ps. 34 Isa. 33. 13–17 Matt. 6. 19–end R ct		G	1 Kings 18. 1–20 Acts 20. 17–end	Ecclus. 3. 17–29 or Ezek. 3. 12–end Mark 13. 14–23 or First EP of Matthew (Ps. 34) Prov. 3. 3–18 Matt. 6. 19–end R ct
EP: Ps. 119. 33–40, 89–96 Eccles. 5. 4–12 Matt. 19. 16–end	**MATTHEW, APOSTLE AND EVANGELIST** Ember Day Isa. 33. 13–17 Ps. 119. 65–72 2 Cor. 4. 1–6 Matt. 9. 9–13	R	(Ps. 49; 117) 1 Kings 19. 15–end 2 Tim. 3. 14–end	(Ps. 119. 33–40, 89–96) Eccles. 5. 4–12 Matt. 19. 16–end
Ps. 65; 66 Ecclus. 4.29 – 6.1 or Ezek. ch. 9 Mark 13. 32–end ct	Ember Day Ember CEG	G	1 Kings ch. 19 Acts 21. 17–36	Ecclus. 4.29 – 6.1 or Ezek. ch. 9 Mark 13. 32–end ct
Ps. 119. 137–152 (or 137–144) Exod. 19. 10–end Matt. 8. 23–end	**THE SEVENTEENTH SUNDAY AFTER TRINITY** Prov. 25. 6–14 Ps. 33. 6–12 Eph. 4. 1–6 Luke 14. 1–11	G	Ps. 119. 153–end Isa. 45. 9–22 Rev. 14. 1–5	Ps. 119. 137–152 (or 137–144) Exod. 19. 10–end Matt. 8. 23–end
Ps. 72; 75 Ecclus. 6. 14–end or Ezek. 10. 1–19 Mark 14. 1–11		G	1 Kings ch. 21 Acts 21.37 – 22.21	Ecclus. 6. 14–end or Ezek. 10. 1–19 Mark 14. 1–11
Ps. 74 Ecclus. 7. 27–end or Ezek. 11. 14–end Mark 14. 12–25		G	1 Kings 22. 1–28 Acts 22.22 – 23.11	Ecclus. 7. 27–end or Ezek. 11. 14–end Mark 14. 12–25

September 2018

			Sunday Principal Service Weekday Eucharist		Third Service Morning Prayer

26	W	Ember Day* *Wilson Carlile, Founder of the Church Army, 1942*			
			Prov. 30. 5–9 Ps. 119. 105–112 Luke 9. 1–6		Ps. 77 1 Kings 22. 29–45 Acts 23. 12–end
	G or R				

27	Th	**Vincent de Paul, Founder of the Congregation of the Mission (Lazarists), 1660**			
		Com. Religious *also* 1 Cor. 1. 25–end Matt. 25. 34–40	*or*	Eccles. 1. 2–11 Ps. 90. 1–6 Luke 9. 7–9	Ps. 78. 1–39† 2 Kings 1. 2–17 Acts 24. 1–23
	Gw				

28	F	Ember Day*			
				Eccles. 3. 1–11 Ps. 144. 1–4 Luke 9. 18–22	Ps. 55 2 Kings 2. 1–18 Acts 24.24 – 25.12
	G or R				

29	Sa	MICHAEL AND ALL ANGELS Ember Day*			
				Gen. 28. 10–17 *or* Rev. 12. 7–12 Ps. 103. 19–end Rev. 12. 7–12 *or* Heb. 1. 5–end John 1. 47–end	MP: Ps. 34; 150 Tobit 12. 6–end *or* Dan. 12. 1–4 Acts 12. 1–11
	W				

30	S	THE EIGHTEENTH SUNDAY AFTER TRINITY **(Proper 21)**			
		Track 1		*Track 2*	
		Esther 7. 1–6, 9–10; 9. 20–22 Ps. 124 James 5. 13–end Mark 9. 38–end		Num. 11. 4–6, 10–16, 24–29 Ps. 19. 7–end James 5. 13–end Mark 9. 38–end	Ps. 122 Isa. 48. 12–end Luke 11. 37–end
	G				

October 2018

1 DEL 26	M	*Remigius, Bishop of Rheims, Apostle of the Franks, 533; Anthony Ashley Cooper, Earl of Shaftesbury,* *Social Reformer, 1885*			
				Job 1. 6–end Ps. 17. 1–11 Luke 9. 46–50	Ps. **80**; 82 2 Kings ch. 5 Acts 26. 1–23
	G				

| **2** | Tu | | | Job 3. 1–3, 11–17, 20–23
Ps. 88. 14–19
Luke 9. 51–56 | Ps. 87; **89.** *1–18*
2 Kings 6. 1–23
Acts 26. 24–end |
| | G | | | | |

3	W	*George Bell, Bishop of Chichester, Ecumenist, Peacemaker, 1958*			
				Job 9. 1–12, 14–16 Ps. 88. 1–6, 11 Luke 9. 57–end	Ps. 119. 105–128 2 Kings 9. 1–16 Acts 27. 1–26
	G				

4	Th	**Francis of Assisi, Friar, Founder of the Friars Minor, 1226**			
		Com. Religious *also* Gal. 6. 14–end Luke 12. 22–34	*or*	Job 19. 21–27a Ps. 27. 13–16 Luke 10. 1–12	Ps. 90; **92** 2 Kings 9. 17–end Acts 27. 27–end
	Gw				

*For Ember Day provision, see p. 11.

Second Service Evening Prayer	Calendar and Holy Communion	Morning Prayer	Evening Prayer
	Cyprian, Bishop of Carthage, Martyr, 258 Com. Martyr		
Ps. 119. 81–104 Ecclus. 10. 6–8, 12–24 or Ezek. 12. 1–16 Mark 14. 26–42	Gr	1 Kings 22. 29–45 Acts 23. 12–end	Ecclus. 10. 6–8, 12–24 or Ezek. 12. 1–16 Mark 14. 26–42
Ps. 78. 40–end† Ecclus. 11. 7–28 or Ezek. 12. 17–end Mark 14. 43–52	G	2 Kings 1. 2–17 Acts 24. 1–23	Ecclus. 11. 7–28 or Ezek. 12. 17–end Mark 14. 43–52
Ps. 69 Ecclus. 14.20 – 15.10 or Ezek. 13. 1–16 Mark 14. 53–65 or First EP of Michael and All Angels Ps. 91 2 Kings 6. 8–17 Matt. 18. 1–6, 10 **W ct**	G	2 Kings 2. 1–18 Acts 24.24 – 25.12	Ecclus. 14.20 – 15.10 or Ezek. 13. 1–16 Mark 14. 53–65 or First EP of Michael and All Angels (Ps. 91) 2 Kings 6. 8–17 John 1. 47–51 **W ct**
	MICHAEL AND ALL ANGELS		
EP: Ps. 138; 148 Dan. 10. 4–end Rev. ch. 5	Dan. 10. 10–19a Ps. 103. 17–22 Rev. 12. 7–12 Matt. 18. 1–10	(Ps. 34; 150) Tobit 12. 6–end or Dan. 12. 1–4 Acts 12. 1–11	(Ps. 138; 148) Gen. 28. 10–17 Rev. ch. 5
	W		
	THE EIGHTEENTH SUNDAY AFTER TRINITY		
Ps. 120; 121 Exod. ch. 24 Matt. 9. 1–8	Deut. 6. 4–9 Ps. 122 1 Cor. 1. 4–8 Matt. 22. 34–end G	Ps. 132 Isa. 48. 12–end Luke 11. 37–end	Ps. 120; 121 Exod. ch. 24 Matt. 9. 1–8
	Remigius, Bishop of Rheims, Apostle of the Franks, 533 Com. Bishop		
Ps. **85**; 86 Ecclus. 16. 17–end or Ezek. 14. 12–end Mark 15. 1–15	Gw	2 Kings ch. 5 Acts 26. 1–23	Ecclus. 16. 17–end or Ezek. 14. 12–end Mark 15. 1–15
Ps. 89. 19–end Ecclus. 17. 1–24 or Ezek. 18. 1–20 Mark 15. 16–32	G	2 Kings 6. 1–23 Acts 26. 24–end	Ecclus. 17. 1–24 or Ezek. 18. 1–20 Mark 15. 16–32
Ps. **91**; 93 Ecclus. 18. 1–14 or Ezek. 18. 21–32 Mark 15. 33–41	G	2 Kings 9. 1–16 Acts 27. 1–26	Ecclus. 18. 1–14 or Ezek. 18. 21–32 Mark 15. 33–41
Ps. 94 Ecclus. 19. 4–17 or Ezek. 20. 1–20 Mark 15. 42–end	G	2 Kings 9. 17–end Acts 27. 27–end	Ecclus. 19. 4–17 or Ezek. 20. 1–20 Mark 15. 42–end

October 2018

		Sunday Principal Service / Weekday Eucharist	Third Service / Morning Prayer

5

F

Job 38. 1, 12–21; 40. 3–5
Ps. 139. 6–11
Luke 10. 13–16

Ps. **88**; (95)
2 Kings 12. 1–19
Acts 28. 1–16

G

6

Sa

William Tyndale, Translator of the Scriptures, Reformation Martyr, 1536
Com. Martyr *or* Job 42. 1–3, 6, 12–end
also Prov. 8. 4–11 Ps. 119. 169–end
2 Tim. 3. 12–end Luke 10. 17–24

Ps. 96; **97**; 100
2 Kings 17. 1–23
Acts 28. 17–end

Gr

7

S

THE NINETEENTH SUNDAY AFTER TRINITY (Proper 22)
Track 1 *Track 2*
Job 1. 1; 2. 1–10 Gen. 2. 18–24
Ps. 26 Ps. 8
Heb. 1. 1–4; 2. 5–12 Heb. 1. 1–4; 2. 5–12
Mark 10. 2–16 Mark 10. 2–16

Ps. 123; 124
Isa. 49. 13–23
Luke 12. 1–12

G

or, if observed as Dedication Festival:

Gen. 28. 11–18
or Rev. 21. 9–14
Ps. 122
1 Pet. 2. 1–10
John 10. 22–29

MP: Ps. 48; 150
Hag. 2. 6–9
Heb. 10. 19–25

ꟺ

8

DEL 27

M

Gal. 1. 6–12
Ps. 111. 1–6
Luke 10. 25–37

Ps. **98**; 99; 101
2 Kings 17. 24–end
Phil. 1. 1–11

G

9

Tu

Denys, Bishop of Paris, and his Companions, Martyrs, c. 250; Robert Grosseteste, Bishop of Lincoln, Philosopher, Scientist, 1253

Gal. 1. 13–end
Ps. 139. 1–9
Luke 10. 38–end

Ps. **106**† (or 103)
2 Kings 18. 1–12
Phil. 1. 12–end

G

10

W

Paulinus, Bishop of York, Missionary, 644
Thomas Traherne, Poet, Spiritual Writer, 1674
Com. Missionary *or* Gal. 2. 1–2, 7–14
esp. Matt. 28. 16–end Ps. 117
Luke 11. 1–4

Ps. 110; **111**; 112
2 Kings 18. 13–end
Phil. 2. 1–13

Gw

11

Th

Ethelburga, Abbess of Barking, 675; James the Deacon, Companion of Paulinus, 7th century
Gal. 3. 1–5
Canticle: Benedictus
Luke 11. 5–13

Ps. 113; **115**
2 Kings 19. 1–19
Phil. 2. 14–end

G

12

F

Wilfrid of Ripon, Bishop, Missionary, 709
Elizabeth Fry, Prison Reformer, 1845; Edith Cavell, Nurse, 1915
Com. Missionary *or* Gal. 3. 7–14
esp. Luke 5. 1–11 Ps. 111. 4–end
also 1 Cor. 1. 18–25 Luke 11. 15–26

Ps. 139
2 Kings 19. 20–36
Phil. 3.1 – 4.1

Gw

13

Sa

Edward the Confessor, King of England, 1066
Com. Saint *or* Gal. 3. 22–end
also 2 Sam. 23. 1–5 Ps. 105. 1–7
1 John 4. 13–16 Luke 11. 27–28

Ps. 120; **121**; 122
2 Kings ch. 20
Phil. 4. 2–end

Gw

Second Service Evening Prayer		Calendar and Holy Communion	Morning Prayer	Evening Prayer
Ps. 102 Ecclus. 19. 20–end or Ezek. 20. 21–38 Mark 16. 1–8	G		2 Kings 12. 1–19 Acts 28. 1–16	Ecclus. 19. 20–end or Ezek. 20. 21–38 Mark 16. 1–8
Ps. 104 Ecclus. 21. 1–17 or Ezek. 24. 15–end Mark 16. 9–end ct or First EP of Dedication Festival: Ps. 24 2 Chron. 7. 11–16 John 4. 19–29 ℣ ct	Gr	**Faith of Aquitaine, Martyr, c. 304** Com. Virgin Martyr	2 Kings 17. 1–23 Acts 28. 17–end	Ecclus. 21. 1–17 or Ezek. 24. 15–end Mark 16. 9–end ct or First EP of Dedication Festival: Ps. 24 2 Chron. 7. 11–16 John 4. 19–29 ℣ ct
Ps. 125; 126 Josh. 3. 7–end Matt. 10. 1–22	G	**THE NINETEENTH SUNDAY AFTER TRINITY** Gen. 18. 23–32 Ps. 141. 1–9 Eph. 4. 17–end Matt. 9. 1–8	Ps. 123; 124 Isa. 49. 13–23 Luke 12. 1–12	Ps. 125; 126 Josh. 3. 7–end Matt. 10. 1–22
EP: Ps. 132 Jer. 7. 1–11 Luke 19. 1–10	℣	or, if observed as Dedication Festival: 2 Chron. 7. 11–16 Ps. 122 1 Cor. 3. 9–17 or 1 Pet. 2. 1–5 Matt. 21. 12–16 or John 10. 22–29	Ps. 48; 150 Hag. 2. 6–9 Heb. 10. 19–25	Ps. 132 Jer. 7. 1–11 Luke 19. 1–10
Ps. 105† (or 103) Ecclus. 22. 6–22 or Ezek. 28. 1–19 John 13. 1–11	G		2 Kings 17. 24–end Phil. 1. 1–11	Ecclus. 22. 6–22 or Ezek. 28. 1–19 John 13. 1–11
Ps. 107† Ecclus. 22.27 – 23.15 or Ezek. 33. 1–20 John 13. 12–20	Gr	**Denys, Bishop of Paris, Martyr, c. 250** Com. Martyr	2 Kings 18. 1–12 Phil. 1. 12–end	Ecclus. 22.27 – 23.15 or Ezek. 33. 1–20 John 13. 12–20
Ps. 119. 129–152 Ecclus. 24. 1–22 or Ezek. 33. 21–end John 13. 21–30	G		2 Kings 18. 13–end Phil. 2. 1–13	Ecclus. 24. 1–22 or Ezek. 33. 21–end John 13. 21–30
Ps. 114; 116; 117 Ecclus. 24. 23–end or Ezek. 34. 1–16 John 13. 31–end	G		2 Kings 19. 1–19 Phil. 2. 14–end	Ecclus. 24. 23–end or Ezek. 34. 1–16 John 13. 31–end
Ps. 130; 131; 137 Ecclus. 27.30 – 28.9 or Ezek. 34. 17–end John 14. 1–14	G		2 Kings 19. 20–36 Phil. 3.1 – 4.1	Ecclus. 27.30 – 28.9 or Ezek. 34. 17–end John 14. 1–14
Ps. 118 Ecclus. 28. 14–end or Ezek. 36. 16–36 John 14. 15–end ct	Gw	**Edward the Confessor, King of England, 1066, translated 1163** Com. Saint	2 Kings ch. 20 Phil. 4. 2–end	Ecclus. 28. 14–end or Ezek. 36. 16–36 John 14. 15–end ct

October 2018

		Sunday Principal Service Weekday Eucharist		Third Service Morning Prayer
14	S	THE TWENTIETH SUNDAY AFTER TRINITY (Proper 23) *Track 1* Job 23. 1–9, 16–end Ps. 22. 1–15 Heb. 4. 12–end	*Track 2* Amos 5. 6–7, 10–15 Ps. 90. 12–end Heb. 4. 12–end	Ps. 129; 130 Isa. 50. 4–10 Luke 13. 22–30
	G	Mark 10. 17–31	Mark 10. 17–31	
15 DEL 28	M	**Teresa of Avila, Teacher, 1582** Com. Teacher *also* Rom. 8. 22–27	*or*	Gal. 4. 21–24, 26–27, 31; 5. 1 Ps. 113 Luke 11. 29–32	Ps. 123; 124; 125; *126* 2 Kings 21. 1–18 1 Tim. 1. 1–17
	Gw			
16	Tu	*Nicholas Ridley, Bishop of London, and Hugh Latimer, Bishop of Worcester, Reformation Martyrs, 1555* 	Gal. 5. 1–6 Ps. 119. 41–48 Luke 11. 37–41	Ps. *132*; 133 2 Kings 22.1 – 22.3 1 Tim. 1.18 – 2.end
	G			
17	W	**Ignatius, Bishop of Antioch, Martyr, c. 107** Com. Martyr *also* Phil. 3. 7–12 John 6. 52–58	*or*	Gal. 5. 18–end Ps. 1 Luke 11. 42–46	Ps. 119. 153–end 2 Kings 23. 4–25 1 Tim. ch. 3
	Gr			
18	Th	LUKE THE EVANGELIST		Isa. 35. 3–6 *or* Acts 16. 6–12a Ps. 147. 1–7 2 Tim. 4. 5–17	MP: Ps. 145; 146 Isa. ch. 55 Luke 1. 1–4
	R		Luke 10. 1–9	
19	F	**Henry Martyn, Translator of the Scriptures, Missionary in India and Persia, 1812** Com. Missionary *esp.* Mark 16. 15–end *also* Isa. 55. 6–11	*or*	Eph. 1. 11–14 Ps. 33. 1–6, 12 Luke 12. 1–7	Ps. 142; *144* 2 Kings 24.18 – 25.12 1 Tim. 5. 1–16
	Gw			
20	Sa		Eph. 1. 15–end Ps. 8 Luke 12. 8–12	Ps. 147 2 Kings 25. 22–end 1 Tim. 5. 17–end
	G			
21	S	THE TWENTY-FIRST SUNDAY AFTER TRINITY (Proper 24) *Track 1* Job 38. 1–7 [34–end] Ps. 104. 1–10, 26, 35c (or 1–10) Heb. 5. 1–10	*Track 2* Isa. 53. 4–end Ps. 91. 9–end Heb. 5. 1–10	Ps. 133; 134; 137. 1–6 Isa. 54. 1–14 Luke 13. 31–end
	G	Mark 10. 35–45	Mark 10. 35–45	
22 DEL 29	M		Eph. 2. 1–10 Ps. 100 Luke 12. 13–21	Ps. *1*; 2; 3 Judith ch. 4 *or* Exod. 22. 21–27; 23. 1–17
	G			1 Tim. 6. 1–10
23	Tu		Eph. 2. 12–end Ps. 85. 7–end Luke 12. 35–38	Ps. *5*; 6; (8) Judith 5.1 – 6.4 *or* Exod. 29.38 – 30.16
	G			1 Tim. 6. 11–end

Second Service Evening Prayer	Calendar and Holy Communion	Morning Prayer	Evening Prayer
	THE TWENTIETH SUNDAY AFTER TRINITY		
Ps. 127; [128] Josh. 5.13 – 6.20 Matt. 11. 20–end	Prov. 9. 1–6 Ps. 145. 15–end Eph. 5. 15–21 **G** Matt. 22. 1–14	Ps. 129; 130 Isa. 50. 4–10 Luke 13. 22–30	Ps. 127; [128] Josh. 5.13 – 6.20 Matt. 11. 20–end
Ps. *127*; 128; 129 Ecclus. 31. 1–11 or Ezek. 37. 1–14 John 15. 1–11	**G**	2 Kings 21. 1–18 1 Tim. 1. 1–17	Ecclus. 31. 1–11 or Ezek. 37. 1–14 John 15. 1–11
Ps. (134); *135* Ecclus. 34. 9–end or Ezek. 37. 15–end John 15. 12–17	**G**	2 Kings 22.1 – 22.3 1 Tim. 1.18 – 2.end	Ecclus. 34. 9–end or Ezek. 37. 15–end John 15. 12–17
Ps. 136 Ecclus. ch. 35 or Ezek. 39. 21–end John 15. 18–end or First EP of Luke Ps. 33 Hos. 6. 1–3 2 Tim. 3. 10–end **R ct**	**Etheldreda, Abbess of Ely, 679** Com. Abbess **Gw**	2 Kings 23. 4–25 1 Tim. ch. 3	Ecclus. ch. 35 or Ezek. 39. 21–end John 15. 18–end or First EP of Luke (Ps. 33) Hos. 6. 1–3 2 Tim. 3. 10–end **R ct**
EP: Ps. 103 Ecclus. 38. 1–14 or Isa. 61. 1–6 Col. 4. 7–end	**LUKE THE EVANGELIST** Isa. 35. 3–6 Ps. 147. 1–6 2 Tim. 4. 5–15 Luke 10. 1–9 **R** or Luke 7. 36–end	(Ps. 145; 146) Isa. ch. 55 Luke 1. 1–4	(Ps. 103) Ecclus. 38. 1–14 or Isa. 61. 1–6 Col. 4. 7–end
Ps. 145 Ecclus. 38. 1–14 or Ezek. 44. 4–16 John 16. 16–22	**G**	2 Kings 24.18 – 25.12 1 Tim. 5. 1–16	Ecclus. 38. 1–14 or Ezek. 44. 4–16 John 16. 16–22
Ps. *148*; 149; 150 Ecclus. 38. 24–end or Ezek. 47. 1–12 John 16. 23–end **ct**	**G**	2 Kings 25. 22–end 1 Tim. 5. 17–end	Ecclus. 38. 24–end or Ezek. 47. 1–12 John 16. 23–end **ct**
	THE TWENTY-FIRST SUNDAY AFTER TRINITY		
Ps. 141 Josh. 14. 6–14 Matt. 12. 1–21	Gen. 32. 24–29 Ps. 90. 1–12 Eph. 6. 10–20 **G** John 4. 46b–end	Ps. 133; 134; 137. 1–6 Isa. 54. 1–14 Luke 13. 31–end	Ps. 142 Josh. 14. 6–14 Matt. 12. 1–21
Ps. *4*; 7 Ecclus. 39. 1–11 or Eccles. ch. 1 John 17. 1–5	**G**	Judith ch. 4 or Exod. 22. 21–27; 23. 1–17 1 Tim. 6. 1–10	Ecclus. 39. 1–11 or Eccles. ch. 1 John 17. 1–5
Ps. *9*; 10† Ecclus. 39. 13–end or Eccles. ch. 2 John 17. 6–19	**G**	Judith 5.1 – 6.4 or Exod. 29.38 – 30.16 1 Tim. 6. 11–end	Ecclus. 39. 13–end or Eccles. ch. 2 John 17. 6–19

October 2018

		Sunday Principal Service Weekday Eucharist	Third Service Morning Prayer

| **24** | W | Eph. 3. 2–12
Ps. 98
Luke 12. 39–48 | Ps. 119. 1–32
Judith 6.10 – 7.7
or Lev. ch. 8 |
| | G | | 2 Tim. 1. 1–14 |

| **25** | Th | *Crispin and Crispinian, Martyrs at Rome, c. 287*
Eph. 3. 14–end
Ps. 33. 1–6
Luke 12. 49–53 | Ps. 14; *15*; 16
Judith 7. 19–end
or Lev. ch. 9 |
| | G | | 2 Tim. 1.15 – 2.13 |

26	F	**Alfred the Great, King of the West Saxons, Scholar, 899** *Cedd, Abbot of Lastingham, Bishop of the East Saxons, 664**	
		Com. Saint *or* Eph. 4. 1–6 *also* 2 Sam. 23. 1–5 Ps. 24. 1–6 John 18. 33–37 Luke 12. 54–end	Ps. 17; *19* Judith 8. 9–end or Lev. 16. 2–24
	Gw		2 Tim. 2. 14–end

27	Sa	Eph. 4. 7–16 Ps. 122 Luke 13. 1–9	Ps. 20; 21; *23* Judith ch. 9 or Lev. ch. 17
			2 Tim. ch. 3
	G		

28	S	**SIMON AND JUDE, APOSTLES** (or transferred to 29 October)** Isa. 28. 14–16 Ps. 119. 89–96 Eph. 2. 19–end John 15. 17–end	MP: Ps. 116; 117 Wisd. 5. 1–16 or Isa. 45. 18–end Luke 6. 12–16
	R		
		or, for The Last Sunday after Trinity (Proper 25): Track 1 Track 2 Job 42. 1–6, 10–end Jer. 31. 7–9 Ps. 34. 1–8, 19–end (*or* 1–8) Ps. 126 Heb. 7. 23–end Heb. 7. 23–end Mark 10. 46–end Mark 10. 46–end	Ps. 119. 89–104 Isa. 59. 9–20 Luke 14. 1–14
		or, if being observed as Bible Sunday: Isa. 55. 1–11 Ps. 19. 7–end 2 Tim. 3.14 – 4.5 John 5. 36b–end	Ps. 119. 89–104 Isa. 45. 22–end Matt. 24. 30–35 or Luke 14. 1–14
	G		

| **29**
DEL 30 | M | **James Hannington, Bishop of Eastern Equatorial Africa, Martyr in Uganda, 1885**
Com. Martyr   *or*   Eph. 4.32 – 5.8
esp. Matt. 10. 28–39   Ps. 1
                           Luke 13. 10–17 | Ps. 27; *30*
Judith ch. 10
or Lev. 19. 1–18, 30–end |
| | Gr | | 2 Tim. 4. 1–8 |

| **30** | Tu | Eph. 5. 21–end
Ps. 128
Luke 13. 18–21 | Ps. 32; *36*
Judith ch. 11
or Lev. 23. 1–22 |
| | G | | 2 Tim. 4. 9–end |

*Chad may be celebrated with Cedd on 26 October instead of 2 March.
**If the Dedication Festival is kept on this Sunday, use the provision given on 6 and 7 October.

Second Service Evening Prayer		Calendar and Holy Communion	Morning Prayer	Evening Prayer
Ps. *11*; 12; 13 Ecclus. 42. 15–end or Eccles. 3. 1–15 John 17. 20–end	G		Judith 6.10 – 7.7 or Lev. ch. 8 2 Tim. 1. 1–14	Ecclus. 42. 15–end or Eccles. 3. 1–15 John 17. 20–end
Ps. 18† Ecclus. 43. 1–12 or Eccles. 3.16 – 4.end John 18. 1–11	Gr	**Crispin, Martyr at Rome, c. 287** Com. Martyr	Judith 7. 19–end or Lev. ch. 9 2 Tim. 1.15 – 2.13	Ecclus. 43. 1–12 or Eccles. 3.16 – 4.end John 18. 1–11
Ps. 22 Ecclus. 43. 13–end or Eccles. ch. 5 John 18. 12–27	G		Judith 8. 9–end or Lev. 16. 2–24 2 Tim. 2. 14–end	Ecclus. 43. 13–end or Eccles. ch. 5 John 18. 12–27
Ps. *24*; 25 Ecclus. 44. 1–15 or Eccles. ch. 6 John 18. 28–end ct or First EP of Simon and Jude Ps. 124; 125; 126 Deut. 32. 1–4 John 14. 15–26 **R ct**	G		Judith ch. 9 or Lev. ch. 17 2 Tim. ch. 3	Ecclus. 44. 1–15 or Eccles. ch. 6 John 18. 28–end ct or First EP of Simon and Jude (Ps. 124; 125; 126) Deut. 32. 1–4 John 14. 15–26 **R ct**
EP: Ps. 119. 1–16 1 Macc. 2. 42–66 or Jer. 3. 11–18 Jude 1–4, 17–end	R	**SIMON AND JUDE, APOSTLES** Isa. 28. 9–16 Ps. 116. 11–end Jude 1–8 or Rev. 21. 9–14 John 15. 17–end *or, for The Twenty-Second Sunday after Trinity:*	Ps. 119. 89–96 Wisd. 5. 1–16 or Isa. 45. 18–end Luke 6. 12–16	Ps. 119. 1–16 1 Macc. 2. 42–66 or Jer. 3. 11–18 Eph. 2. 19–end
Ps. 119. 121–136 Eccles. chs 11 and 12 2 Tim. 2. 1–7 *Gospel:* Luke 18. 9–14		Gen. 45. 1–7, 15 Ps. 133 Phil. 1. 3–11 Matt. 18. 21–end	Ps. 119. 89–104 Isa. 59. 9–20 Luke 14. 1–14	Ps. 119. 121–136 Eccles. chs 11 and 12 2 Tim. 2. 1–7
Ps. 119. 1–16 2 Kings ch. 22 Col. 3. 12–17 *Gospel:* Luke 4. 14–30	G			
Ps. 26; *28*; 29 Ecclus. 44.19 – 45.5 or Eccles. 7. 1–14 John 19. 1–16	G		Judith ch. 10 or Lev. 19. 1–18, 30–end 2 Tim. 4. 1–8	Ecclus. 44.19 – 45.5 or Eccles. 7. 1–14 John 19. 1–16
Ps. 33 Ecclus. 45. 6–17 or Eccles. 7. 15–end John 19. 17–30	G		Judith ch. 11 or Lev. 23. 1–22 2 Tim. 4. 9–end	Ecclus. 45. 6–17 or Eccles. 7. 15–end John 19. 17–30

October 2018

			Sunday Principal Service Weekday Eucharist	Third Service Morning Prayer
31	W	Martin Luther, Reformer, 1546	Eph. 6. 1–9 Ps. 145. 10–20 Luke 13. 22–30	Ps. 34 Judith ch. 12 or Lev. 23. 23–end Titus ch. 1
	G			

November 2018

1	Th	**ALL SAINTS' DAY**		Wisd. 3. 1–9 or Isa. 25. 6–9 Ps. 24. 1–6 Rev. 21. 1–6a	MP: Ps. 15; 84; 149 Isa. ch. 35 Luke 9. 18–27
	ꝟ			John 11. 32–44	
		or, if the readings above are used on Sunday 4 November:		Isa. 56. 3–8 or 2 Esdras 2. 42–end Ps. 33. 1–5 Heb. 12. 18–24	MP: Ps. 111; 112; 117 Wisd. 5. 1–16 or Jer. 31. 31–34 2 Cor. 4. 5–12
	ꝟ			Matt. 5. 1–12	
		or, if kept as a feria:		Eph. 6. 10–20 Ps. 144. 1–2, 9–11 Luke 13. 31–end	Ps. 37† Judith ch. 13 or Lev. 24. 1–9
	G				Titus ch. 2
2	F	**Commemoration of the Faithful Departed (All Souls' Day)**		Lam. 3. 17–26, 31–33 or or Wisd. 3. 1–9 Ps. 23 or Ps. 27. 1–6, 16–end Rom. 5. 5–11 or 1 Pet. 1. 3–9 John 5. 19–25 or John 6. 37–40	Phil. 1. 1–11 Ps. 111 Luke 14. 1–6	Ps. 31 Judith 15. 1–13 or Lev. 25. 1–24 Titus ch. 3
	Rp or Gp				
3	Sa	**Richard Hooker, Priest, Anglican Apologist, Teacher, 1600** Martin of Porres, Friar, 1639			
		Com. Teacher or esp. John 16. 12–15 also Ecclus. 44. 10–15		Phil. 1. 18–26 Ps. 42. 1–7 Luke 14. 1, 7–11	Ps. 41; **42**; 43 Judith 15.14 – 16.end or Num. 6. 1–5, 21–end Philemon
	Rw or Gw				
4	S	THE FOURTH SUNDAY BEFORE ADVENT		Deut. 6. 1–9 Ps. 119. 1–8 Heb. 9. 11–14 Mark 12. 28–34	Ps. 112; 149 Jer. 31. 31–34 1 John 3. 1–3
	R or G				
	ꝟ	or ALL SAINTS' SUNDAY (see readings for 1 November throughout the day)			

Second Service Evening Prayer	Calendar and Holy Communion	Morning Prayer	Evening Prayer
First EP of All Saints Ps. 1; 5 Ecclus. 44. 1–15 *or* Isa. 40. 27–end Rev. 19. 6–10 🙏 **ct** *or, if All Saints is observed on 4 November:* Ps. 119. 33–56 Ecclus. 46. 1–10 *or* Eccles. ch. 8 John 19. 31–end	**G**	Judith ch. 12 *or* Lev. 23. 23–end Titus ch. 1	*First EP of All Saints* Ps. 1; 5 Ecclus. 44. 1–15 *or* Isa. 40. 27–end Rev. 19. 6–10 🙏 **ct**
	ALL SAINTS' DAY		
EP: Ps. 148; 150 Isa. 65. 17–end Heb. 11.32 – 12.2	Isa. 66. 20–23 Ps. 33. 1–5 Rev. 7. 2–4 [5–8] 9–12 Matt. 5. 1–12	Ps. 15; 84; 149 Isa. ch. 35 Luke 9. 18–27	Ps. 148; 150 Isa. 65. 17–end Heb. 11.32 – 12.2
EP: Ps. 145 Isa. 66. 20–23 Col. 1. 9–14			
Ps. 39; **40** Ecclus. 50. 1–24 *or* Eccles. ch. 9 John 20. 1–10	🙏		
	To celebrate All Souls' Day, see *Common Worship* provision.		
Ps. 35 Ecclus. 51. 1–12 *or* Eccles. 11. 1–8 John 20. 11–18		Judith 15. 1–13 *or* Lev. 25. 1–24 Titus ch. 3	Ecclus. 51. 1–12 *or* Eccles. 11. 1–8 John 20. 11–18
	G		
Ps. 45; **46** Ecclus. 51. 13–end *or* Eccles. 11.9 – 12.end John 20. 19–end **ct**	**G**	Judith 15.14 – 16.end *or* Num. 6. 1–5, 21–end Philemon	Ecclus. 51. 13–end *or* Eccles. 11.9 – 12.end John 20. 19–end **ct**
	THE TWENTY-THIRD SUNDAY AFTER TRINITY		
Ps. 145 (*or* 145. 1–9) Dan. 2. 1–48 (*or* 1–11, 25–48) Rev. 7. 9–end *Gospel:* Matt. 5. 1–12	Isa. 11. 1–10 Ps. 44. 1–9 Phil. 3. 17–end Matt. 22. 15–22	Ps. 112; 149 Jer. 31. 31–34 1 John 3. 1–3	Ps. 145 (*or* 145. 1–9) Dan. 2. 1–48 (*or* 1–11, 25–48) Rev. 7. 9–end
	G		

November 2018

5 DEL 31	M R or G		Phil. 2. 1–4 Ps. 131 Luke 14. 12–14	Ps. **2**; 146 alt. Ps. 44 Dan. ch. 1 Rev. ch. 1
6	Tu R or G	Leonard, Hermit, 6th century; William Temple, Archbishop of Canterbury, Teacher, 1944	Phil. 2. 5–11 Ps. 22. 22–27 Luke 14. 15–24	Ps. **5**; 147. 1–12 alt. Ps. **48**; 52 Dan. 2. 1–24 Rev. 2. 1–11
7	W **Willibrord of York, Bishop, Apostle of Frisia, 739** Com. Missionary esp. Isa. 52. 7–10 Matt. 28. 16–end Rw or Gw	or	Phil. 2. 12–18 Ps. 27. 1–5 Luke 14. 25–33	Ps. **9**; 147. 13–end alt. Ps. 119. 57–80 Dan. 2. 25–end Rev. 2. 12–end
8	Th **The Saints and Martyrs of England** Isa. 61. 4–9 or Ecclus. 44. 1–15 Ps. 15 Rev. 19. 5–10 John 17. 18–23 Rw or Gw	or	Phil. 3. 3–8a Ps. 105. 1–7 Luke 15. 1–10	Ps. 11; **15**; 148 alt. Ps. 56; **57**; (63†) Dan. 3. 1–18 Rev. 3. 1–13
9	F R or G	Margery Kempe, Mystic, c. 1440	Phil. 3.17 – 4.1 Ps. 122 Luke 16. 1–8	Ps. **16**; 149 alt. Ps. **51**; 54 Dan. 3. 19–end Rev. 3. 14–end
10	Sa **Leo the Great, Bishop of Rome, Teacher, 461** Com. Teacher also 1 Pet. 5. 1–11 Rw or Gw	or	Phil. 4. 10–19 Ps. 112 Luke 16. 9–15	Ps. **18**. **31–end**; 150 alt. Ps. 68 Dan. 4. 1–18 Rev. ch. 4
11	S THE THIRD SUNDAY BEFORE ADVENT (Remembrance Sunday) R or G		Jonah 3. 1–5, 10 Ps. 62. 5–end Heb. 9. 24–end Mark 1. 14–20	Ps. 136 Mic. 4. 1–5 Phil. 4. 6–9
12 DEL 32	M R or G		Titus 1. 1–9 Ps. 24. 1–6 Luke 17. 1–6	Ps. 19; **20** alt. Ps. 71 Dan. 4. 19–end Rev. ch. 5
13	Tu **Charles Simeon, Priest, Evangelical Divine, 1836** Com. Pastor esp. Mal. 2. 5–7 also Col. 1. 3–8 Luke 8. 4–8 Rw or Gw	or	Titus 2. 1–8, 11–14 Ps. 37. 3–5, 30–32 Luke 17. 7–10	Ps. **21**; 24 alt. Ps. 73 Dan. 5. 1–12 Rev. ch. 6
14	W R or G	Samuel Seabury, first Anglican Bishop in North America, 1796	Titus 3. 1–7 Ps. 23 Luke 17. 11–19	Ps. **23**; 25 alt. Ps. 77 Dan. 5. 13–end Rev. 7. 1–4, 9–end
15	Th R or G		Philemon 7–20 Ps. 146. 4–end Luke 17. 20–25	Ps. **26**; 27 alt. Ps. 78. 1–39† Dan. ch. 6 Rev. ch. 8

Second Service Evening Prayer		Calendar and Holy Communion	Morning Prayer	Evening Prayer
Ps. 92; 96; 97 alt. Ps. 47; 49 Isa. 1. 1–20 Matt. 1. 18–end	G		Dan. ch. 1 Rev. ch. 1	Isa. 1. 1–20 Matt. 1. 18–end
Ps. 98; 99; 100 alt. Ps. 50 Isa. 1. 21–end Matt. 2. 1–15	Gw	**Leonard, Hermit, 6th century** Com. Abbot	Dan. 2. 1–24 Rev. 2. 1–11	Isa. 1. 21–end Matt. 2. 1–15
Ps. 111; 112; 116 alt. Ps. 59; 60; (67) Isa. 2. 1–11 Matt. 2. 16–end	G		Dan. 2. 25–end Rev. 2. 12–end	Isa. 2. 1–11 Matt. 2. 16–end
Ps. 118 alt. Ps. 61; 62; 64 Isa. 2. 12–end Matt. ch. 3	G		Dan. 3. 1–18 Rev. 3. 1–13	Isa. 2. 12–end Matt. ch. 3
Ps. 137; 138; 143 alt. Ps. 38 Isa. 3. 1–15 Matt. 4. 1–11	G		Dan. 3. 19–end Rev. 3. 14–end	Isa. 3. 1–15 Matt. 4. 1–11
Ps. 145 alt. Ps. 65; 66 Isa. 4.2 – 5.7 Matt. 4. 12–22 ct	G		Dan. 4. 1–18 Rev. ch. 4	Isa. 4.2 – 5.7 Matt. 4. 12–22 ct
		THE TWENTY-FOURTH SUNDAY AFTER TRINITY		
Ps. 46; [82] Isa. 10.33 – 11.9 John 14. 1–29 (or 23–29)	G	Isa. 55. 6–11 Ps. 85. 1–7 Col. 1. 3–12 Matt. 9. 18–26	Ps. 136 Mic. 4. 1–5 Phil. 4. 6–9	Ps. 144 Isa. 10.33 – 11.9 John 14. 1–29 (or 23–29)
Ps. 34 alt. Ps. 72; 75 Isa. 5. 8–24 Matt. 4.23 – 5.12	G		Dan. 4. 19–end Rev. ch. 5	Isa. 5. 8–24 Matt. 4.23 – 5.12
Ps. 36; 40 alt. Ps. 74 Isa. 5. 25–end Matt. 5. 13–20	Gw	**Britius, Bishop of Tours, 444** Com. Bishop	Dan. 5. 1–12 Rev. ch. 6	Isa. 5. 25–end Matt. 5. 13–20
Ps. 37 alt. Ps. 119. 81–104 Isa. ch. 6 Matt. 5. 21–37	G		Dan. 5. 13–end Rev. 7. 1–4, 9–end	Isa. ch. 6 Matt. 5. 21–37
Ps. 42; 43 alt. Ps. 78. 40–end† Isa. 7. 1–17 Matt. 5. 38–end	Gw	**Machutus, Bishop, Apostle of Brittany, c. 564** Com. Bishop	Dan. ch. 6 Rev. ch. 8	Isa. 7. 1–17 Matt. 5. 38–end

November 2018

			Sunday Principal Service Weekday Eucharist	Third Service Morning Prayer

16 F **Margaret, Queen of Scotland, Philanthropist, Reformer of the Church, 1093**
Edmund Rich of Abingdon, Archbishop of Canterbury, 1240

Com. Saint	or	2 John 4–9	Ps. 28; **32**
also Prov. 31. 10–12, 20, 26–end		Ps. 119. 1–8	*alt.* Ps. 55
1 Cor. 12.13 – 13.3		Luke 17. 26–end	Dan. 7. 1–14
Matt. 25. 34–end			Rev. 9. 1–12

Rw or **Gw**

17 Sa **Hugh, Bishop of Lincoln, 1200**

Com. Bishop	or	3 John 5–8	Ps. 33
also 1 Tim. 6. 11–16		Ps. 112	*alt.* Ps. **76**; 79
		Luke 18. 1–8	Dan. 7. 15–end
			Rev. 9. 13–end

Rw or **Gw**

18 S THE SECOND SUNDAY BEFORE ADVENT

Dan. 12. 1–3	Ps. 96
Ps. 16	1 Sam. 9.27 – 10.2a;
Heb. 10. 11–14 [15–18] 19–25	10. 17–26
Mark 13. 1–8	Matt. 13. 31–35

R or **G**

19 M **Hilda, Abbess of Whitby, 680**
DEL 33 *Mechtild, Béguine of Magdeburg, Mystic, 1280*

Com. Religious	or	Rev. 1. 1–4; 2. 1–5	Ps. 46; **47**
esp. Isa. 61.10 – 62.5		Ps. 1	*alt.* Ps. **80**; 82
		Luke 18. 35–end	Dan. 8. 1–14
			Rev. ch. 10

Rw or **Gw**

20 Tu **Edmund, King of the East Angles, Martyr, 870**
Priscilla Lydia Sellon, a Restorer of the Religious Life in the Church of England, 1876

Com. Martyr	or	Rev. 3. 1–6, 14–end	Ps. 48; **52**
also Prov. 20. 28; 21. 1–4, 7		Ps. 15	*alt.* Ps. 87; **89. 1–18**
		Luke 19. 1–10	Dan. 8. 15–end
			Rev. 11. 1–14

R or **Gr**

21 W

Rev. ch. 4	Ps. **56**; 57
Ps. 150	*alt.* Ps. 119. 105–128
Luke 19. 11–28	Dan. 9. 1–19
	Rev. 11. 15–end

R or **G**

22 Th *Cecilia, Martyr at Rome, c. 230*

Rev. 5. 1–10	Ps. 61; **62**
Ps. 149. 1–5	*alt.* Ps. 90; **92**
Luke 19. 41–44	Dan. 9. 20–end
	Rev. ch. 12

R or **G**

23 F **Clement, Bishop of Rome, Martyr, c. 100**

Com. Martyr	or	Rev. 10. 8–end	Ps. **63**; 65
also Phil. 3.17 – 4.3		Ps. 119. 65–72	*alt.* Ps. **88**; (95)
Matt. 16. 13–19		Luke 19. 45–end	Dan. 10.1 – 11.1
			Rev. 13. 1–10

R or **Gr**

24 Sa

Rev. 11. 4–12	Ps. 78. 1–39
Ps. 144. 1–9	*alt.* Ps. 96; **97**; 100
Luke 20. 27–40	Dan. ch. 12
	Rev. 13. 11–end

R or **G**

25 S CHRIST THE KING
The Sunday Next Before Advent

Dan. 7. 9–10, 13–14	MP: Ps. 29; 110
Ps. 93	Isa. 32. 1–8
Rev. 1. 4b–8	Rev. 3. 7–end
John 18. 33–37	

R or **W**

Second Service Evening Prayer	Calendar and Holy Communion	Morning Prayer	Evening Prayer
Ps. 31 *alt.* Ps. 69 Isa. 8. 1–15 Matt. 6. 1–18 **G**		Dan. 7. 1–14 Rev. 9. 1–12	Isa. 8. 1–15 Matt. 6. 1–18
Ps. 84; **86** *alt.* Ps. 81; **84** Isa. 8.16 – 9.7 Matt. 6. 19–end **ct** **Gw**	**Hugh, Bishop of Lincoln, 1200** Com. Bishop	Dan. 7. 15–end Rev. 9. 13–end	Isa. 8.16 – 9.7 Matt. 6. 19–end **ct**
Ps. 95 Dan. ch. 3 (*or* 3. 13–end) Matt. 13. 24–30, 36–43 **G**	**THE TWENTY-FIFTH SUNDAY AFTER TRINITY** 1 Sam. 10. 17–24 Ps. 97 Rom. 13.1–7 Matt. 8. 23–34	Ps. 96 1 Sam. 9.27 – 10.2a; 10. 17–26 Matt. 13. 31–35	Ps. 95 Dan. ch. 3 (*or* 3. 13–end) Matt. 13. 24–30, 36–43
Ps. 70; **71** *alt.* Ps. **85**; 86 Isa. 9.8 – 10.4 Matt. 7. 1–12 **G**		Dan. 8. 1–14 Rev. ch. 10	Isa. 9.8 – 10.4 Matt. 7. 1–12
Ps. **67**; 72 *alt.* Ps. 89. 19–end Isa. 10. 5–19 Matt. 7. 13–end **Gr**	**Edmund, King of the East Angles, Martyr, 870** Com. Martyr	Dan. 8. 15–end Rev. 11. 1–14	Isa. 10. 5–19 Matt. 7. 13–end
Ps. 73 *alt.* Ps. **91**; 93 Isa. 10. 20–32 Matt. 8. 1–13 **G**		Dan. 9. 1–19 Rev. 11. 15–end	Isa. 10. 20–32 Matt. 8. 1–13
Ps. 74; **76** *alt.* Ps. 94 Isa. 10.33 – 11.9 Matt. 8. 14–22 **Gr**	**Cecilia, Martyr at Rome, c. 230** Com. Virgin Martyr	Dan. 9. 20–end Rev. ch. 12	Isa. 10.33 – 11.9 Matt. 8. 14–22
Ps. 77 *alt.* Ps. 102 Isa. 11.10 – 12.end Matt. 8. 23–end **Gr**	**Clement, Bishop of Rome, Martyr, c. 100** Com. Martyr	Dan. 10.1 – 11.1 Rev. 13. 1–10	Isa. 11.10 – 12.end Matt. 8. 23–end
Ps. 78. 40–end *alt.* Ps. 104 Isa. 13. 1–13 Matt. 9. 1–17 **ct** *or First EP of Christ the King* Ps. 99; 100 Isa. 10.33 – 11.9 1 Tim. 6. 11–16 **R** *or* **W ct** **G**		Dan. ch. 12 Rev. 13. 11–end	Isa. 13. 1–13 Matt. 9. 1–17 **ct**
EP: Ps. 72 (*or* 72. 1–7) Dan. ch. 5 John 6. 1–15	**THE SUNDAY NEXT BEFORE ADVENT** To celebrate Christ the King, see *Common Worship* provision. Jer. 23. 5–8 Ps. 85. 8–end Col. 1. 13–20 John 6. 5–14 **G**	Ps. 29; 110 Isa. 32. 1–8 Rev. 3. 7–end	Ps. 72 (*or* 72. 1–7) Dan. ch. 5 Rev. 1. 4b–8

November 2018

		Sunday Principal Service / Weekday Eucharist	Third Service / Morning Prayer

26 M
DEL 34

R or G

Rev. 14. 1–5
Ps. 24. 1–6
Luke 21. 1–4

Ps. 92; *96*
alt. Ps. *98*; 99; 101
Isa. 40. 1–11
Rev. 14. 1–13

27 Tu

R or G

Rev. 14. 14–19
Ps. 96
Luke 21. 5–11

Ps. *97*; 98; 100
alt. Ps. *106*† (or 103)
Isa. 40. 12–26
Rev. 14.14 – 15.end

28 W

R or G

Rev. 15. 1–4
Ps. 98
Luke 21. 12–19

Ps. 110; 111; *112*
alt. Ps. 110; *111*; 112
Isa. 40.27 – 41.7
Rev. 16. 1–11

29 Th

Rev. 18. 1–2, 21–23; 19. 1–3, 9
Ps. 100
Luke 21. 20–28

Ps. *125*; 126; 127; 128
alt. Ps. 113; *115*
Isa. 41. 8–20
Rev. 16. 12–end

Day of Intercession and Thanksgiving for the Missionary Work of the Church

R or G

Isa. 49. 1–6; Isa. 52. 7–10; Mic. 4. 1–5
Ps. 2; 46; 47
Acts 17. 12–end; 2 Cor. 5.14 – 6.2; Eph. 2. 13–end
Matt. 5. 13–16; Matt. 28. 16–end; John 17. 20–end

30 F   **ANDREW THE APOSTLE**

R

Isa. 52. 7–10
Ps. 19. 1–6
Rom. 10. 12–18
Matt. 4. 18–22

MP: Ps. 47; 147. 1–12
Ezek. 47. 1–12
or Ecclus. 14. 20–end
John 12. 20–32

December 2018

1 Sa   *Charles de Foucauld, Hermit in the Sahara, 1916*

R or G

Rev. 22. 1–7
Ps. 95. 1–7
Luke 21. 34–36

Ps. 145
alt. Ps. 120; *121*; 122
Isa. 42. 10–17
Rev. ch. 18

2 S   **THE FIRST SUNDAY OF ADVENT**
CW Year C begins

P

Jer. 33. 14–16
Ps. 25. 1–9
1 Thess. 3. 9–end
Luke 21. 25–36

Ps. 44
Isa. 51. 4–11
Rom. 13. 11–end

3 M   *Francis Xavier, Missionary, Apostle of the Indies, 1552*
Daily Eucharistic Lectionary Year 1 begins

P

Isa. 2. 1–5
Ps. 122
Matt. 8. 5–11

Ps. *50*; 54
alt. Ps. *1*; 2; 3
Isa. 42. 18–end
Rev. ch. 19

4 Tu   *John of Damascus, Monk, Teacher, c. 749; Nicholas Ferrar, Deacon, Founder of the Little Gidding Community, 1637*

P

Isa. 11. 1–10
Ps. 72. 1–4, 18–19
Luke 10. 21–24

Ps. *80*; 82
alt. Ps. *5*; 6; (8)
Isa. 43. 1–13
Rev. ch. 20

Second Service Evening Prayer		Calendar and Holy Communion	Morning Prayer	Evening Prayer
Ps. *80*; 81 *alt.* Ps. 105† (*or* 103) Isa. 14. 3–20 Matt. 9. 18–34	G		Isa. 40. 1–11 Rev. 14. 1–13	Isa. 14. 3–20 Matt. 9. 18–34
Ps. 99; *101* *alt.* Ps. 107† Isa. ch. 17 Matt. 9.35 – 10.15	G		Isa. 40. 12–26 Rev. 14.14 – 15.end	Isa. ch. 17 Matt. 9.35 – 10.15
Ps. 121; *122*; 123; 124 *alt.* Ps. 119. 129–152 Isa. ch. 19 Matt. 10. 16–33	G		Isa. 40.27 – 41.7 Rev. 16. 1–11	Isa. ch. 19 Matt. 10. 16–33
Ps. 131; 132; *133* *alt.* Ps. 114; *116*; 117 Isa. 21. 1–12 Matt. 10.34 – 11.1 *or First EP of Andrew the Apostle* Ps. 48 Isa. 49. 1–9a 1 Cor. 4. 9–16			Isa. 41. 8–20 Rev. 16. 12–end	Isa. 21. 1–12 Matt. 10.34 – 11.1 *or First EP of Andrew* *the Apostle* (Ps. 48) Isa. 49. 1–9a 1 Cor. 4. 9–16 **R** ct
		To celebrate the Day of Intercession and Thanksgiving for the Missionary Work of the Church, see *Common Worship* provision.		
R ct	G			
EP: Ps. 87; 96 Zech. 8. 20–end John 1. 35–42	R	**ANDREW THE APOSTLE** Zech. 8. 20–end Ps. 92. 1–5 Rom. 10. 9–end Matt. 4. 18–22	(Ps. 47; 147. 1–12) Ezek. 47. 1–12 *or* Ecclus. 14. 20–end John 12. 20–32	(Ps. 87; 96) Isa. 52. 7–10 John 1. 35–42
Ps. 148; 149; *150* *alt.* Ps. 118 Isa. ch. 24 Matt. 11. 20–end **P** ct	G		Isa. 42. 10–17 Rev. ch. 18	Isa. ch. 24 Matt. 11. 20–end **P** ct
Ps. 9 (*or* 9. 1–8) Joel 3. 9–end Rev. 14.13 – 15.4 *Gospel:* John 3. 1–17	P	**THE FIRST SUNDAY IN ADVENT** Advent 1 Collect until Christmas Eve Mic. 4. 1–4, 6–7 Ps. 25. 1–9 Rom. 13. 8–14 Matt. 21. 1–13	Ps. 44 Isa. 51. 4–11 Rom. 13. 11–end	Ps. 9 (*or* 9. 1–8) Joel 3. 9–end Rev. 14.13 – 15.4
Ps. 70; *71* *alt.* Ps. *4*; 7 Isa. 25. 1–9 Matt. 12. 1–21	P		Isa. 42. 18–end Rev. ch. 19	Isa. 25. 1–9 Matt. 12. 1–21
Ps. *74*; 75 *alt.* Ps. *9*; 10† Isa. 26. 1–13 Matt. 12. 22–37	P		Isa. 43. 1–13 Rev. ch. 20	Isa. 26. 1–13 Matt. 12. 22–37

December 2018

			Sunday Principal Service Weekday Eucharist	Third Service Morning Prayer
5	W		Isa. 25. 6–10a Ps. 23 Matt. 15. 29–37	Ps. 5; **7** alt. Ps. 119. 1–32 Isa. 43. 14–end
	P			Rev. 21. 1–8
6	Th	**Nicholas, Bishop of Myra, c. 326** Com. Bishop or also Isa. 61. 1–3 1 Tim. 6. 6–11	Isa. 26. 1–6 Ps. 118. 18–27a Matt. 7. 21, 24–27	Ps. **42**; 43 alt. Ps. 14; **15**; 16 Isa. 44. 1–8
	Pw	Mark 10. 13–16		Rev. 21. 9–21
7	F	**Ambrose, Bishop of Milan, Teacher, 397** Com. Teacher or also Isa. 41. 9b–13 Luke 22. 24–30	Isa. 29. 17–end Ps. 27. 1–4, 16–17 Matt. 9. 27–31	Ps. **25**; 26 alt. Ps. 17; **19** Isa. 44. 9–23
	Pw			Rev. 21.22 – 22.5
8	Sa	**The Conception of the Blessed Virgin Mary** Com. BVM or	Isa. 30. 19–21, 23–26 Ps. 146. 4–9 Matt. 9.35 – 10.1, 6–8	Ps. **9**; (10) alt. Ps. 20; 21; **23** Isa. 44.24 – 45.13
	Pw			Rev. 22. 6–end
9	S	THE SECOND SUNDAY OF ADVENT	Baruch ch. 5 or Mal. 3. 1–4 Canticle: Benedictus Phil. 1. 3–11	Ps. 80 Isa. 64. 1–7 Matt. 11. 2–11
	P		Luke 3. 1–6	
10	M		Isa. ch. 35 Ps. 85. 7–end Luke 5. 17–26	Ps. 44 alt. Ps. 27; **30** Isa. 45. 14–end
	P			1 Thess. ch. 1
11	Tu		Isa. 40. 1–11 Ps. 96. 1, 10–end Matt. 18. 12–14	Ps. **56**; 57 alt. Ps. 32; **36** Isa. ch. 46
	P			1 Thess. 2. 1–12
12	W	Ember Day*	Isa. 40. 25–end Ps. 103. 8–13 Matt. 11. 28–end	Ps. **62**; 63 alt. Ps. 34 Isa. ch. 47
	P			1 Thess. 2. 13–end
13	Th	**Lucy, Martyr at Syracuse, 304** Samuel Johnson, Moralist, 1784 Com. Martyr or also Wisd. 3. 1–7 2 Cor. 4. 6–15	Isa. 41. 13–20 Ps. 145. 1, 8–13 Matt. 11. 11–15	Ps. 53; **54**; 60 alt. Ps. 37† Isa. 48. 1–11
	Pr			1 Thess. ch. 3
14	F	**John of the Cross, Poet, Teacher, 1591** Ember Day* Com. Teacher or esp. 1 Cor. 2. 1–10 also John 14. 18–23	Isa. 48. 17–19 Ps. 1 Matt. 11. 16–19	Ps. 85; **86** alt. Ps. 31 Isa. 48. 12–end
	Pw			1 Thess. 4. 1–12
15	Sa	Ember Day*	Ecclus. 48. 1–4, 9–11 or 2 Kings 2. 9–12 Ps. 80. 1–4, 18–19 Matt. 17. 10–13	Ps. 145 alt. Ps. 41; **42**; 43 Isa. 49. 1–13
	P			1 Thess. 4. 13–end

*For Ember Day provision, see p. 11.

Second Service Evening Prayer	Calendar and Holy Communion	Morning Prayer	Evening Prayer
Ps. 76; *77* *alt.* Ps. *11*; 12; 13 Isa. 28. 1–13 Matt. 12. 38–end	P	Isa. 43. 14–end Rev. 21. 1–8	Isa. 28. 1–13 Matt. 12. 38–end
Ps. *40*; 46 *alt.* Ps. 18† Isa. 28. 14–end Matt. 13. 1–23	**Nicholas, Bishop of Myra, *c.* 326** Com. Bishop Pw	Isa. 44. 1–8 Rev. 21. 9–21	Isa. 28. 14–end Matt. 13. 1–23
Ps. 16; *17* *alt.* Ps. 22 Isa. 29. 1–14 Matt. 13. 24–43	P	Isa. 44. 9–23 Rev. 21.22 – 22.5	Isa. 29. 1–14 Matt. 13. 24–43
Ps. *27*; 28 *alt.* Ps. *24*; 25 Isa. 29. 15–end Matt. 13. 44–end ct	**The Conception of the Blessed Virgin Mary** Isa. 44.24 – 45.13 Rev. 22. 6–end Pw	Isa. 29. 15–end Matt. 13. 44–end ct
Ps. 75; [76] Isa. 40. 1–11 Luke 1. 1–25	THE SECOND SUNDAY IN ADVENT 2 Kings 22. 8–10; 23. 1–3 Ps. 50. 1–6 Rom. 15. 4–13 Luke 21. 25–33 P	Ps. 40 Isa. 64. 1–7 Luke 3. 1–6	Ps. 75 [76] Mal. 3. 1–4 Luke 1. 1–25
Ps. *144*; 146 *alt.* Ps. 26; *28*; 29 Isa. 30. 1–18 Matt. 14. 1–12	P	Isa. 45. 14–end 1 Thess. ch. 1	Isa. 30. 1–18 Matt. 14. 1–12
Ps. *11*; 12; 13 *alt.* Ps. 33 Isa. 30. 19–end Matt. 14. 13–end	P	Isa. ch. 46 1 Thess. 2. 1–12	Isa. 30. 19–end Matt. 14. 13–end
Ps. *10*; 14 *alt.* Ps. 119. 33–56 Isa. ch. 31 Matt. 15. 1–20	P	Isa. ch. 47 1 Thess. 2. 13–end	Isa. ch. 31 Matt. 15. 1–20
Ps. 73 *alt.* Ps. 39; *40* Isa. ch. 32 Matt. 15. 21–28	**Lucy, Martyr at Syracuse, 304** Com. Virgin Martyr Pr	Isa. 48. 1–11 1 Thess. ch. 3	Isa. ch. 32 Matt. 15. 21–28
Ps. 82; *90* *alt.* Ps. 35 Isa. 33. 1–22 Matt. 15. 29–end	P	Isa. 48. 12–end 1 Thess. 4. 1–12	Isa. 33. 1–22 Matt. 15. 29–end
Ps. 93; *94* *alt.* Ps. 45; *46* Isa. ch. 35 Matt. 16. 1–12 ct	P	Isa. 49. 1–13 1 Thess. 4. 13–end	Isa. ch. 35 Matt. 16. 1–12 ct

December 2018

			Sunday Principal Service Weekday Eucharist	Third Service Morning Prayer
16	S	THE THIRD SUNDAY OF ADVENT		
			Zeph. 3. 14–end Canticle: Isa. 12. 2–6 or Ps. 146. 4–end Phil. 4. 4–7	Ps. 12; 14 Isa. 25. 1–9 1 Cor. 4. 1–5
	P		Luke 3. 7–18	
17	M	O Sapientia Eglantyne Jebb, Social Reformer, Founder of 'Save the Children', 1928		
			Gen. 49. 2, 8–10 Ps. 72. 1–5, 18–19 Matt. 1. 1–17	Ps. 40 alt. Ps. 44 Isa. 49. 14–25
	P			1 Thess. 5. 1–11
18	Tu		Jer. 23. 5–8 Ps. 72. 1–2, 12–13, 18–end Matt. 1. 18–24	Ps. 70; 74 alt. Ps. 48; 52 Isa. ch. 50
	P			1 Thess. 5. 12–end
19	W		Judg. 13. 2–7, 24–end Ps. 71. 3–8 Luke 1. 5–25	Ps. 144; 146 Isa. 51. 1–8 2 Thess. ch. 1
	P			
20	Th		Isa. 7. 10–14 Ps. 24. 1–6 Luke 1. 26–38	Ps. 46; 95 Isa. 51. 9–16 2 Thess. ch. 2
	P			
21	F	*	Zeph. 3. 14–18 Ps. 33. 1–4, 11–12, 20–end Luke 1. 39–45	Ps. 121; 122; 123 Isa. 51. 17–end 2 Thess. ch. 3
	P			
22	Sa		1 Sam. 1. 24–end Ps. 113 Luke 1. 46–56	Ps. 124; 125; 126; 127 Isa. 52. 1–12 Jude
	P			
23	S	THE FOURTH SUNDAY OF ADVENT	Mic. 5. 2–5a Canticle: Magnificat or Ps. 80. 1–8 Heb. 10. 5–10	Ps. 144 Isa. 32. 1–8 Rev. 22. 6–end
	P		Luke 1. 39–45 [46–55]	
24	M	CHRISTMAS EVE	Morning Eucharist 2 Sam. 7. 1–5, 8–11, 16 Ps. 89. 2, 19–27 Acts 13. 16–26	Ps. 45; 113 Isa. 52.13 – 53.end 2 Pet. 1. 1–15
	P		Luke 1. 67–79	

*Thomas the Apostle may be celebrated on 21 December instead of 3 July.

Second Service Evening Prayer	Calendar and Holy Communion		Morning Prayer	Evening Prayer
	THE THIRD SUNDAY IN ADVENT			
	O Sapientia			
Ps. 50. 1–6; [62]	Isa. ch. 35		Ps. 12; 14	Ps. 62
Isa. ch. 35	Ps. 80. 1–7		Isa. 25. 1–9	Zeph. 3. 14–end
Luke 1. 57–66 [67–end]	1 Cor. 4. 1–5		Luke 3. 7–18	Luke 1. 57–66
	Matt. 11. 2–10			[67–end]
		P		
Ps. 25; **26**			Isa. 49. 14–25	Isa. 38. 1–8, 21–22
alt. Ps. **47**; 49			1 Thess. 5. 1–11	Matt. 16. 13–end
Isa. 38. 1–8, 21–22				
Matt. 16. 13–end		P		
Ps. **50**; 54			Isa. ch. 50	Isa. 38. 9–20
alt. Ps. 50			1 Thess. 5. 12–end	Matt. 17. 1–13
Isa. 38. 9–20				
Matt. 17. 1–13		P		
	Ember Day			
Ps. 10; **57**	Ember CEG		Isa. 51. 1–8	Isa. ch. 39
Isa. ch. 39			2 Thess. ch. 1	Matt. 17. 14–21
Matt. 17. 14–21		P		
Ps. **4**; 9			Isa. 51. 9–16	Zeph. 1.1 – 2.3
Zeph. 1.1 – 2.3			2 Thess. ch. 2	Matt. 17. 22–end
Matt. 17. 22–end				*or First EP of Thomas*
				(Ps. 27)
				Isa. ch. 35
				Heb. 10.35 – 11.1
		P		R ct
	THOMAS THE APOSTLE			
	Ember Day			
Ps. 80; **84**	Job 42. 1–6		(Ps. 92; 146)	(Ps. 139)
Zeph. 3. 1–13	Ps. 139. 1–11		2 Sam. 15. 17–21	Hab. 2. 1–4
Matt. 18. 1–20	Eph. 2. 19–end		*or Ecclus. ch. 2*	1 Pet. 1. 3–12
	John 20. 24–end	R	John 11. 1–16	
	Ember Day			
Ps. 24; **48**	Ember CEG		Isa. 52. 1–12	Zeph. 3. 14–end
Zeph. 3. 14–end			Jude	Matt. 18. 21–end
Matt. 18. 21–end				
ct		P		ct
	THE FOURTH SUNDAY IN ADVENT			
Ps. 123; [131]	Isa. 40. 1–9		Ps. 144	Ps. 123; [131]
Isa. 10.33 – 11.10	Ps. 145. 17–end		Isa. 32. 1–8	Isa. 10.33 – 11.10
Matt. 1. 18–end	Phil. 4. 4–7		Rev. 22. 6–end	Matt. 1. 18–end
	John 1. 19–28			
		P		
	CHRISTMAS EVE			
Ps. 85	Collect (1) Christmas Eve		Isa. 52.13 – 53.end	Zech. ch. 2
Zech. ch. 2	(2) Advent 1		2 Pet. 1. 1–15	Rev. 1. 1–8
Rev. 1. 1–8	Mic. 5. 2–5a			
	Ps. 24			
	Titus 3. 3–7			
	Luke 2. 1–14	P		

December 2018

		Sunday Principal Service Weekday Eucharist	Third Service Morning Prayer
25	Tu	**CHRISTMAS DAY** *Any of the following sets of readings may be used on the evening of Christmas Eve and on Christmas Day. Set III should be used at some service during the celebration.* ℘	*I* Isa. 9. 2–7 Ps. 96 Titus 2. 11–14 Luke 2. 1–14 [15–20] *II* Isa. 62. 6–end Ps. 97 Titus 3. 4–7 Luke 2. [1–7] 8–20 *III* Isa. 52. 7–10 Ps. 98 Heb. 1. 1–4 [5–12] John 1. 1–14	MP: Ps. *110*; 117 Isa. 62. 1–5 Matt. 1. 18–end
26	W R	STEPHEN, DEACON, FIRST MARTYR	2 Chron. 24. 20–22 *or* Acts 7. 51–end Ps. 119. 161–168 Acts 7. 51–end *or* Gal. 2. 16b–20 Matt. 10. 17–22	MP: Ps. *13*; 31. 1–8; 150 Jer. 26. 12–15 Acts ch. 6
27	Th W	JOHN, APOSTLE AND EVANGELIST	Exod. 33. 7–11a Ps. 117 1 John ch. 1 John 21. 19b–end	MP: Ps. *21*; 147. 13–end Exod. 33. 12–end 1 John 2. 1–11
28	F R	THE HOLY INNOCENTS	Jer. 31. 15–17 Ps. 124 1 Cor. 1. 26–29 Matt. 2. 13–18	MP: Ps. *36*; 146 Baruch 4. 21–27 *or* Gen. 37. 13–20 Matt. 18. 1–10
29	Sa Wr	**Thomas Becket, Archbishop of Canterbury, Martyr, 1170*** Com. Martyr *or* *esp.* Matt. 10. 28–33 *also* Ecclus. 51. 1–8	1 John 2. 3–11 Ps. 96. 1–4 Luke 2. 22–35	Ps. *19*; 20 Isa. 57. 15–end John 1. 1–18
30	S W	THE FIRST SUNDAY OF CHRISTMAS	1 Sam. 2. 18–20, 26 Ps. 148 (*or* 148. 1–6) Col. 3. 12–17 Luke 2. 41–end	Ps. 105. 1–11 Isa. 41.21 – 42.1 1 John 1. 1–7
31	M W	*John Wyclif, Reformer, 1384*	1 John 2. 18–21 Ps. 96. 1, 11–end John 1. 1–18	Ps. 102 Isa. 59. 15b–end John 1. 29–34

---

*Thomas Becket may be celebrated on 7 July instead of 29 December.

Second Service Evening Prayer		Calendar and Holy Communion	Morning Prayer	Evening Prayer
EP: Ps. 8 Isa. 65. 17–25 Phil. 2. 5–11 or Luke 2. 1–20 *if it has not been used at the* *principal service of the day*		**CHRISTMAS DAY** Isa. 9. 2–7 Ps. 98 Heb. 1. 1–12 John 1. 1–14	Ps. 110; 117 Isa. 62. 1–5 Matt. 1. 18–end	Ps. 8 Isa. 65. 17–25 Phil. 2. 5–11 or Luke 2. 1–20
	℟			
EP: Ps. 57; *86* Gen. 4. 1–10 Matt. 23. 34–end		**STEPHEN, DEACON, FIRST MARTYR** Collect (1) Stephen (2) Christmas 2 Chron. 24. 20–22 Ps. 119. 161–168 Acts 7. 55–end	(Ps. 13; 31. 1–8; 150) Jer. 26. 12–15 Acts ch. 6	(Ps. 57; 86) Gen. 4. 1–10 Matt. 10. 17–22
	R	Matt. 23. 34–end		
EP: Ps. 97 Isa. 6. 1–8 1 John 5. 1–12		**JOHN, APOSTLE AND EVANGELIST** Collect (1) John (2) Christmas Exod. 33. 18–end Ps. 92. 11–end 1 John ch. 1	(Ps. 21; 147. 13–end) Exod. 33. 7–11a 1 John 2. 1–11	(Ps. 97) Isa. 6. 1–8 1 John 5. 1–12
	W	John 21. 19b–end		
EP: Ps. 123; *128* Isa. 49. 14–25 Mark 10. 13–16		**THE HOLY INNOCENTS** Collect (1) Innocents (2) Christmas Jer. 31. 10–17 Ps. 123 Rev. 14. 1–5	(Ps. 36; 146) Baruch 4. 21–27 *or* Gen. 37. 13–20 Matt. 18. 1–10	(Ps. 124; 128) Isa. 49. 14–25 Mark 10. 13–16
	R	Matt. 2. 13–18		
Ps. 131; *132* Jonah ch. 1 Col. 1. 1–14 ct		CEG of Christmas	Isa. 57. 15–end John 1. 1–18	Jonah ch. 1 Col. 1. 1–14
	W			ct
Ps. 132 Isa. ch. 61 Gal. 3.27 – 4.7 *Gospel:* Luke 2. 15–21		**THE SUNDAY AFTER CHRISTMAS DAY** Isa. 62. 10–12 Ps. 45. 1–7 Gal. 4. 1–7	Ps. 105. 1–11 Isa. 41.21 – 42.1 1 John 1. 1–7	Ps. 132 Isa. ch. 61 Luke 2. 15–21
	W	Matt. 1. 18–end		
Ps. *90*; 148 Jonah chs 3 & 4 Col. 1.24 – 2.7 *or First EP of The Naming* *of Jesus* Ps. 148 Jer. 23. 1–6 Col. 2. 8–15 ct		**Silvester, Bishop of Rome, 335** Com. Bishop	Isa. 59. 15b–end John 1. 29–34	Jonah chs 3 & 4 Col. 1.24 – 2.7 *or First EP of The* *Circumcision of Christ* (Ps. 148) Jer. 23. 1–6 Col. 2. 8–15
	W			ct

The *Common Worship* Additional Weekday Lectionary

The Additional Weekday Lectionary provides two readings on a one-year cycle for each day (except for Sundays, Principal Feasts and Holy Days, Festivals and Holy Week). They 'stand alone' and are intended particularly for use in those churches and cathedrals that attract occasional rather than regular congregations. The Additional Weekday Lectionary has been designed to complement rather than replace the existing Weekday Lectionary. Thus a church with a regular congregation in the morning and a congregation made up mainly of visitors in the evening would continue to use the Weekday Lectionary in the morning but might choose to use this Additional Weekday Lectionary for Evening Prayer.

Psalms are not provided, since the Weekday Lectionary already offers a variety of approaches with regard to psalmody. This Lectionary is not intended for use at the Eucharist; the Daily Eucharistic Lectionary is already authorized for that purpose.

On Sundays, Principal Feasts, other Principal Holy Days, Festivals, and in Holy Week, where no readings are provided in this table, the lectionary provision in the main part of this volume should be used.

Date	Old Testament	New Testament	Date	Old Testament	New Testament
December 2017				Isa. 41. 14–20	John 1. 29–34
3 S	THE FIRST SUNDAY OF ADVENT			*Where The Epiphany is celebrated on Sunday*	
4 M	Mal. 3. 1–6	Matt. 3. 1–6		*7 January, The Baptism of Christ is transferred*	
5 Tu	Zeph. 3. 14–end	1 Thess. 4. 13–end		*to Monday 8 January.*	
6 W	Isa. 65.17 – 66.2	Matt. 24. 1–14	9 Tu	Exod. 17. 1–7	Acts 8. 26–end
7 Th	Mic. 5. 2–5a	John 3. 16–21	10 W	Exod. 15. 1–19	Col. 2. 8–15
8 F	Isa. 66. 18–end	Luke 13. 22–30	11 Th	Zech. 6. 9–15	1 Pet. 2. 4–10
9 Sa	Mic. 7. 8–15	Rom. 15.30 – 16.7, 25–end	12 F	Isa. 51. 7–16	Gal. 6. 14–18
			13 Sa	Lev. 16. 11–22	Heb. 10. 19–25
10 S	THE SECOND SUNDAY OF ADVENT		14 S	THE SECOND SUNDAY OF EPIPHANY	
11 M	Jer. 7. 1–11	Phil. 4. 4–9	15 M	1 Kings. 17. 8–16	Mark 8. 1–10
12 Tu	Dan. 7. 9–14	Matt. 24. 15–28	16 Tu	1 Kings 19. 1–9a	Mark 1. 9–15
13 W	Amos 9. 11–end	Rom. 13. 8–14	17 W	1 Kings 19. 9b–18	Mark 9. 2–13
14 Th	Jer. 23. 5–8	Mark 11. 1–11	18 Th	Lev. 11. 1–8, 13–19, 41–45	Acts 10. 9–16
15 F	Jer. 33. 14–22	Luke 21. 25–36	19 F	Isa. 49. 8–13	Acts 10. 34–43
16 Sa	Zech. 14. 4–11	Rev. 22. 1–7	20 Sa	Gen. 35. 1–15	Acts 10. 44–end
17 S	THE THIRD SUNDAY OF ADVENT		21 S	THE THIRD SUNDAY OF EPIPHANY	
18 M	Exod. 3. 1–6	Acts 7. 20–36	22 M	Ezek. 37. 15–end	John 17. 1–19
19 Tu	Isa. 11. 1–9	Rom. 15. 7–13	23 Tu	Ezek. 20. 39–44	John 17. 20–end
20 W	Isa. 22. 21–23	Rev. 3. 7–13	24 W	Neh. 2. 1–10	Rom. 12. 1–8
21 Th	Num. 24. 15b–19	Rev. 22. 10–21	25 Th	THE CONVERSION OF PAUL	
22 F	Jer. 30. 7–11a	Acts 4. 1–12	26 F	Lev. 19. 9–28	Rom. 15. 1–7
23 Sa	Isa. 7. 10–15	Matt. 1. 18–23	27 Sa	Jer. 33. 1–11	1 Pet. 5. 5b–end
24 S	THE FOURTH SUNDAY OF ADVENT (Christmas Eve)			*or, where The Presentation is celebrated on Sunday*	
25 M	**CHRISTMAS DAY**			*28 January, First EP of Presentation of Christ*	
26 Tu	STEPHEN		28 S	THE FOURTH SUNDAY OF EPIPHANY (or *The Presentation*)	
27 W	JOHN THE EVANGELIST		29 M	Jonah ch. 3	2 Cor. 5. 11–21
28 Th	THE HOLY INNOCENTS		30 Tu	Prov. 4. 10–end	Matt. 5. 13–20
29 F	Mic. 1. 1–4; 2. 12–13	Luke 2. 1–7	31 W	Isa. 61. 1–9	Luke 7. 18–30
30 Sa	Isa. 9. 2–7	John 8. 12–20			
31 S	THE FIRST SUNDAY OF CHRISTMAS		**February 2018**		
			1 Th	Isa. 52. 1–12	Matt. 10. 1–15
January 2018			2 F	**THE PRESENTATION** or	
1 M	**NAMING AND CIRCUMCISION OF JESUS**			Isa. 56. 1–8	Matt. 28. 16–end
2 Tu	Isa. 66. 6–14	Matt. 12. 46–50	3 Sa	Hab. 2. 1–4	Rev. 14. 1–7
3 W	Deut. 6. 4–15	John 10. 31–end	4 S	THE SECOND SUNDAY BEFORE LENT	
4 Th	Isa. 63. 7–16	Gal. 3.23 – 4.7	5 M	Isa. 61. 1–9	Mark 6. 1–13
5 F	*At Evening Prayer, the readings for the Eve of Epiphany*		6 Tu	Isa. 52. 1–10	Rom. 10. 5–21
	are used. At other services, or where, for pastoral		7 W	Isa. 52.13 – 53.6	Rom. 15. 14–21
	reasons, The Epiphany is celebrated on Sunday		8 Th	Isa. 53. 4–12	2 Cor. 4. 1–10
	7 January, the following readings are used:		9 F	Zech. 8. 16–end	Matt. 10. 1–15
	Isa. ch. 12	2 Cor. 2. 12–end	10 Sa	Jer. 1. 4–10	Matt. 10. 16–22
6 Sa	**THE EPIPHANY**		11 S	THE SUNDAY NEXT BEFORE LENT	
	Where The Epiphany is celebrated on Sunday 7 January,		12 M	2 Kings 2. 13–22	3 John
	the readings for the Eve of The Epiphany are used		13 Tu	Judges 14. 5–17	Rev. 10. 4–11
	at Evening Prayer. Where The Baptism of Christ is		14 W	**ASH WEDNESDAY**	
	celebrated on Sunday 7 January, the readings for the		15 Th	Gen. 2. 7–end	Heb. 2. 5–end
	Eve of The Baptism of Christ are used at Evening		16 F	Gen. 4. 1–12	Heb. 4. 12–end
	Prayer. At other services, the following readings		17 Sa	2 Kings 22. 11–end	Heb. 5. 1–10
	are used:		18 S	THE FIRST SUNDAY OF LENT	
	Gen. 25. 19–end	Eph. 1. 1–6	19 M	Gen. 6. 11–end; 7. 11–16	Luke 4. 14–21
7 S	THE BAPTISM OF CHRIST (The First Sunday of Epiphany)		20 Tu	Deut. 31. 7–13	1 John 3. 1–10
8 M	*Where The Epiphany is celebrated on Saturday*		21 W	Gen. 11. 1–9	Matt. 24. 15–28
	6 January and the Baptism of Christ on Sunday		22 Th	Gen. 13. 1–13	1 Pet. 2. 13–end
	7 January, these readings are used on Monday 8 January:		23 F	Gen. 21. 1–8	Luke 9. 18–27
			24 Sa	Gen. 32. 22–32	2 Pet. 1. 10–end

Date		Old Testament	New Testament
25	S	THE SECOND SUNDAY OF LENT	
26	M	1 Chron. 21. 1–17	1 John 2. 1–8
27	Tu	Zech. ch. 3	2 Pet. 2. 1–10a
28	W	Job. 1. 1–22	Luke 21.34 – 22.6

March 2018

Date		Old Testament	New Testament
1	Th	2 Chron. 29. 1–11	Mark 11. 15–19
2	F	Exod. 19. 1–9a	1 Pet. 1. 1–9
3	Sa	Exod. 19. 9b–19	Acts 7. 44–50
4	S	THE THIRD SUNDAY OF LENT	
5	M	Josh. 4. 1–13	Luke 9. 1–11
6	Tu	Exod. 15. 2–27	Heb. 10. 32–end
7	W	Gen. 9. 8–17	1 Pet. 3. 18–end
8	Th	Dan. 12. 5–end	Mark 13. 21–end
9	F	Num. 20. 1–13	1 Cor. 10. 23–end
10	Sa	Isa. 43. 14–end	Heb. 3. 1–15
11	S	THE FOURTH SUNDAY OF LENT (Mothering Sunday)	
12	M	2 Kings 24.18 – 25.7	1 Cor. 15. 20–34
13	Tu	Jer. 13. 12–19	Acts 13. 26–35
14	W	Jer. 13. 20–27	1 Pet. 1.17 – 2.3
15	Th	Jer. 22. 11–19	Luke 11. 37–52
16	F	Jer. 17. 1–14	Luke 6. 17–26
17	Sa	Ezra ch. 1	2 Cor. 1. 12–19
18	S	THE FIFTH SUNDAY OF LENT (Passiontide begins)	
19	M	JOSEPH OF NAZARETH	
20	Tu	Isa. 58. 1–14	Mark 10. 32–45
21	W	Joel 36. 1–12	John 14. 1–14
22	Th	Jer. 9. 17–22	Luke 13. 31–35
23	F	Lam. 5. 1–3, 19–22	John 12. 20–26
24	Sa	Job 17. 6–end	John 12. 27–36
25	S	PALM SUNDAY	
		HOLY WEEK	

April 2018

Date		Old Testament	New Testament
1	S	EASTER DAY	
2	M	Isa. 54. 1–14	Rom. 1. 1–7
3	Tu	Isa. 51. 1–11	John 5. 19–29
4	W	Isa. 26. 1–19	John 20. 1–10
5	Th	Isa. 43. 14–21	Rev. 1. 4–end
6	F	Isa. 42. 10–17	1 Thess. 5. 1–11
7	Sa	Job 14. 1–14	John 21. 1–14
8	S	THE SECOND SUNDAY OF EASTER	
9	M	THE ANNUNCIATION (transferred from 25 March)	
10	Tu	Prov. 8. 1–11	Acts 16. 6–15
11	W	Hos. 5.15 – 6.6	1 Cor. 15. 1–11
12	Th	Jonah ch. 2	Mark 4. 35–end
13	F	Gen. 6. 9–end	1 Pet. 3. 8–end
14	Sa	1 Sam. 2. 1–8	Matt. 28. 8–15
15	S	THE THIRD SUNDAY OF EASTER	
16	M	Exod. 24. 1–11	Rev. ch. 5
17	Tu	Lev. 19. 9–18, 32–end	Matt. 5. 38–end
18	W	Gen. 3. 8–21	1 Cor. 15. 12–28
19	Th	Isa. 33. 13–22	Mark 6. 47–end
20	F	Neh. 9. 6–17	Rom. 5. 12–end
21	Sa	Isa. 61.10 – 62.5	Luke 24. 1–12
22	S	THE FOURTH SUNDAY OF EASTER	
23	M	GEORGE	
24	Tu	Job 31. 13–23	Matt. 7. 1–12
25	W	MARK	
26	Th	Prov. 28. 3–end	Mark 10. 17–31
27	F	Eccles. 12. 1–8	Rom. 6. 1–11
28	Sa	1 Chron. 29. 10–13	Luke 24. 13–35
29	S	THE FIFTH SUNDAY OF EASTER	
30	M	Gen. 15. 1–18	Rom. 4. 13–end

May 2018

Date		Old Testament	New Testament
1	Tu	PHILIP AND JAMES	
2	W	Hos. 13. 4–14	1 Cor. 15. 50–end
3	Th	Exod. 3. 1–15	Mark 12. 18–27
4	F	Ezek. 36. 33–end	Rom. 8. 1–11
5	Sa	Isa. 38. 9–20	Luke 24. 33–end
6	S	THE SIXTH SUNDAY OF EASTER	
7	M	Prov. 4. 1–13	Phil. 2. 1–11
8	Tu	Isa. 32. 12–end	Rom. 5. 1–11
9	W	At Evening Prayer, the readings for the Eve of Ascension Day are used. At other services, the following readings are used:	
		Isa. 43. 1–13	Titus 2.11 – 3.8
10	Th	ASCENSION DAY	
11	F	Exod. 35.30 – 36.1	Gal. 5. 13–end
12	Sa	Num. 11. 16–17, 24–29	1 Cor. ch. 2
13	S	THE SEVENTH SUNDAY OF EASTER (Sunday after Ascension Day)	
14	M	MATTHIAS	
		Where Matthias is celebrated on 24 February:	
		Num. 27. 15–end	1 Cor. ch. 3
15	Tu	1 Sam. 10. 1–10	1 Cor. 12. 1–13
16	W	1 Kings 19. 1–18	Matt. 3. 13–end
17	Th	Ezek. 11. 14–20	Matt. 9. 35 – 10.20
18	F	Ezek. 36. 22–28	Matt. 12. 22–32
19	Sa	At Evening Prayer, the readings for the Eve of Pentecost are used. At other services, the following readings are used:	
		Mic. 3. 1–8	Eph. 6. 10–20
20	S	PENTECOST (Whit Sunday)	
21	M	Gen. 12. 1–9	Rom. 4. 13–end
22	Tu	Gen. 13. 1–12	Rom. 12. 9–end
23	W	Gen. ch. 15	Rom. 4. 1–8
24	Th	Gen. 22. 1–18	Heb. 11. 8–19
25	F	Isa. 51. 1–8	John 8. 48–end
26	Sa	At Evening Prayer, the readings for the Eve of Trinity Sunday are used. At other services, the following readings are used:	
		Ecclus. 44. 19–23 or	James 2. 14–26
		Josh. 2. 1–15	
27	S	TRINITY SUNDAY	
28	M	Exod. 2. 1–10	Heb. 11. 23–31
29	Tu	Exod. 2. 11–end	Acts 7. 17–29
30	W	Exod. 3. 1–12	Acts 7. 30–38
31	Th	Day of Thanksgiving for the Institution of Holy Communion (Corpus Christi), or The Visitation, or, where Corpus Christi is celebrated as a Lesser Festival and The Visitation kept on 2 July:	
		Exod. 6. 1–13	John 9. 24–38

June 2018

Date		Old Testament	New Testament
1	F	Exod. 34. 1–10	Mark 7. 1–13
2	Sa	Exod. 34. 27–end	2 Cor. 3. 7–end
3	S	THE FIRST SUNDAY AFTER TRINITY	
4	M	Gen. 37. 1–11	Rom. 11. 9–21
5	Tu	Gen. 41. 15–40	Mark 13. 1–13
6	W	Gen. 42. 17–end	Matt. 18. 1–14
7	Th	Gen. 45. 1–15	Acts 7. 9–16
8	F	Gen. 47. 1–12	1 Thess. 5. 12–end
9	Sa	Gen. 50. 4–21	Luke 15. 11–end
10	S	THE SECOND SUNDAY AFTER TRINITY	
11	M	BARNABAS	
12	Tu	Prov. 3. 1–18	Matt. 5. 1–12
13	W	Judg. 6. 1–16	Matt. 5. 13–24
14	Th	Jer. 6. 9–15	1 Tim. 2. 1–6
15	F	1 Sam. 16. 14–end	John 14. 15–end
16	Sa	Isa. 6. 1–9	Rev. 19. 9–end
17	S	THE THIRD SUNDAY AFTER TRINITY	
18	M	Exod. 13. 13b–end	Luke 15. 1–10
19	Tu	Prov. 1. 20–end	James 5. 13–end

Date		Old Testament	New Testament
20	W	Isa. 5. 8–24	James 1. 17–25
21	Th	Isa. 57. 14–end	John 13. 1–17
22	F	Jer. 15. 15–end	Luke 16. 19–31
23	Sa	Isa. 25. 1–9	Acts 2. 22–33
24	S	THE BIRTH OF JOHN THE BAPTIST (THE FOURTH SUNDAY AFTER TRINITY)	
25	M	Exod. 20. 1–17	Matt. 6. 1–15
26	Tu	Prov. 6. 6–19	Luke 4. 1–14
27	W	Isa. 24. 1–15	1 Cor. 6. 1–11
28	Th	Job ch. 7	Matt. 7. 21–29
29	F	PETER AND PAUL	
30	Sa	Job ch. 28	Heb. 11.32 – 12.2

July 2018

1	S	THE FIFTH SUNDAY AFTER TRINITY	
2	M	Exod. 32. 1–14	Col. 3. 1–11
3	Tu	THOMAS	
		Where Thomas is celebrated on 21 December:	
		Prov. 9. 1–12	2 Thess. 2.13 – 3.5
4	W	Isa. 26. 1–9	Rom. 8. 12–27
5	Th	Jer. 8.18 – 9.6	John 13. 21–35
6	F	2 Sam. 5. 1–12	Matt. 27. 45–56
7	Sa	Hos. 11. 1–11	Matt. 28. 1–7
8	S	THE SIXTH SUNDAY AFTER TRINITY	
9	M	Exod. 40. 1–16	Luke 14. 15–24
10	Tu	Prov. 11. 1–12	Mark 12. 38–44
11	W	Isa. 33. 2–10	Phil. 1. 1–11
12	Th	Job ch. 38	Luke 18. 1–14
13	F	Job 42. 1–6	John 3. 1–15
14	Sa	Eccles. 9. 1–11	Heb. 1. 1–9
15	S	THE SEVENTH SUNDAY AFTER TRINITY	
16	M	Num. 23. 1–12	1 Cor. 1. 10–17
17	Tu	Prov. 12. 1–12	Gal. 3. 1–14
18	W	Isa. 49. 8–13	2 Cor. 8. 1–11
19	Th	Hos. ch. 14	John 15. 1–17
20	F	2 Sam. 18. 18–end	Matt. 27. 57–66
21	Sa	Isa. 55. 1–7	Mark 16. 1–8
22	S	MARY MAGDALENE (THE EIGHTH SUNDAY AFTER TRINITY)	
23	M	Joel 3. 16–21	Mark 4. 21–34
24	Tu	Prov. 12. 13–end	John 1. 43–51
25	W	JAMES	
26	Th	Isa. 38. 1–8	Mark 5. 21–43
27	F	Jer. 14. 1–9	Luke 8. 4–15
28	Sa	Eccles. 5. 10–19	1 Tim. 6. 6–16
29	S	THE NINTH SUNDAY AFTER TRINITY	
30	M	Josh. 1. 1–9	1 Cor. 9. 19–end
31	Tu	Prov. 15. 1–11	Gal. 2. 15–end

August 2018

1	W	Isa. 49. 1–7	1 John ch. 1
2	Th	Prov. 27. 1–12	John 15. 12–27
3	F	Isa. 59. 8–end	Mark 15. 6–20
4	Sa	Zech. 7.8 – 8.8	Luke 20. 27–40
5	S	THE TENTH SUNDAY AFTER TRINITY	
6	M	THE TRANSFIGURATION	
7	Tu	Prov. 15. 15–end	Matt. 15. 21–28
8	W	Isa. 45. 1–7	Eph. 4. 1–16
9	Th	Jer. 16. 1–15	Luke 12. 35–48
10	F	Jer. 18. 1–11	Heb. 1. 1–9
11	Sa	Jer. 26. 1–19	Eph. 3. 1–13
12	S	THE ELEVENTH SUNDAY AFTER TRINITY	
13	M	Ruth 2. 1–13	Luke 10. 25–37
14	Tu	Prov. 16. 1–11	Phil. 3. 4b–end
15	W	THE BLESSED VIRGIN MARY	
		Where the Blessed Virgin Mary is celebrated on 8 September:	
		Deut. 11. 1–21	2 Cor. 9. 6–end

Date		Old Testament	New Testament
16	Th	Ecclus. ch. 2 *or* Eccles. 2. 12–25	John 16. 1–15
17	F	Obad. 1–10	John 19. 1–16
18	Sa	2 Kings 2. 11–14	Luke 24. 36–end
19	S	THE TWELFTH SUNDAY AFTER TRINITY	
20	M	1 Sam. 17. 32–50	Matt. 8. 14–22
21	Tu	Prov. 17. 1–15	Luke 7. 1–17
22	W	Jer. 5. 20–end	2 Pet. 3. 8–end
23	Th	Dan. 2. 1–23	Luke 10. 1–20
24	F	BARTHOLOMEW	
25	Sa	Dan. ch. 6	Phil. 2. 14–24
26	S	THE THIRTEENTH SUNDAY AFTER TRINITY	
27	M	2 Sam. 7. 4–17	2 Cor. 5. 1–10
28	Tu	Prov. 18. 10–21	Rom. 14. 10–end
29	W	Judg. 4. 1–10	Rom. 1. 8–17
30	Th	Isa. 49. 14–end	John 16. 16–24
31	F	Job 9. 1–24	Mark 15. 21–32

September 2018

1	Sa	Exod. 19. 1–9	John 20. 11–18
2	S	THE FOURTEENTH SUNDAY AFTER TRINITY	
3	M	Hag. ch. 1	Mark 7. 9–23
4	Tu	Prov. 21. 1–18	Mark 6. 30–44
5	W	Hos. 11. 1–11	1 John 4. 9–end
6	Th	Lam. 3. 34–48	Rom. 7. 14–end
7	F	1 Kings 19. 4–18	1 Thess. ch. 3
8	Sa	Ecclus. 4. 11–28 *or* Deut. 29. 2–15	2 Tim. 3. 10–end
9	S	THE FIFTEENTH SUNDAY AFTER TRINITY	
10	M	Wisd. 6. 12–21 *or* Job 12. 1–16	Matt. 15. 1–9
11	Tu	Prov. 8. 1–11	Luke 6. 39–end
12	W	Prov. 2. 1–15	Col. 1. 9–20
13	Th	Baruch 3. 14–end *or* Gen. 1. 1–13	John 1. 1–18
14	F	HOLY CROSS DAY	
15	Sa	Wisd. 9. 1–12 *or* Jer. 1. 4–10	Luke 2. 41–end
16	S	THE SIXTEENTH SUNDAY AFTER TRINITY	
17	M	Gen. 21. 1–13	Luke 1. 26–38
18	Tu	Ruth 4. 7–17	Luke 2. 25–38
19	W	2 Kings 4. 1–7	John 2. 1–11
20	Th	2 Kings 4. 25b–37	Mark 3. 19b–35
21	F	MATTHEW	
22	Sa	Exod. 15. 19–27	Acts 1. 6–14
23	S	THE SEVENTEENTH SUNDAY AFTER TRINITY	
24	M	Exod. 19. 16–end	Heb. 12. 18–end
25	Tu	1 Chron. 16. 1–13	Rev. 11. 15–end
26	W	1 Chron. 29. 10–19	Col. 3. 12–17
27	Th	Neh. 8. 1–12	1 Cor. 14. 1–12
28	F	Isa. 1. 10–17	Mark 12. 28–34
29	Sa	MICHAEL AND ALL ANGELS	
30	S	THE EIGHTEENTH SUNDAY AFTER TRINITY	

October 2018

1	M	2 Sam. 22. 4–7, 17–20	Heb. 7.26 – 8.6
2	Tu	Prov. 22. 17–end	2 Cor. 12. 1–10
3	W	Hos. ch. 14	James 2. 14–26
4	Th	Isa. 24. 1–15	John 16. 25–33
5	F	Jer. 14. 1–9	Luke 23. 44–56
6	Sa	Zech. 8. 14–end	John 20. 19–end
7	S	THE NINETEENTH SUNDAY AFTER TRINITY	
8	M	1 Kings 3. 3–14	1 Tim. 3.13 – 4.8
9	Tu	Prov. 27. 11–end	Gal. 6. 1–10
10	W	Isa. 51. 1–6	2 Cor. 1. 1–11
11	Th	Ecclus. 18. 1–14 *or* Job ch. 26	1 Cor. 11. 17–end
12	F	Ecclus. 28. 2–12 *or*	Mark 15. 33–37

Date		Old Testament	New Testament
		Job 19. 21–end	
13	Sa	Isa. 44. 21–end	John 21. 15–end
14	S	THE TWENTIETH SUNDAY AFTER TRINITY	
15	M	I Kings 6. 2–10	John 12. 1–11
16	Tu	Prov. 31. 10–end	Luke 10. 38–42
17	W	Jonah ch. 1	Luke 5. 1–11
18	Th	LUKE	
19	F	Isa. ch. 64	Matt. 27. 45–56
20	Sa	2 Sam. 7. 18–end	Acts 2. 22–33
21	S	THE TWENTY-FIRST SUNDAY AFTER TRINITY	
22	M	I Kings 8. 22–30	John 12. 12–19
23	Tu	Eccles. ch. 11	Luke 13. 10–17
24	W	Hos. 14. 1–7	2 Tim. 4. 1–8
25	Th	Isa. 49. 1–7	John 19. 16–25a
26	F	Prov. 24. 3–22	John 8. 1–11
27	Sa	Ecclus. 7. 8–17, 32–end or Deut. 6. 16–25	2 Tim. 1. 1–14
28	S	SIMON AND JUDE (THE LAST SUNDAY AFTER TRINITY)	
29	M	Isa. 42. 14–21	Luke 1. 5–25
30	Tu	I Sam. 4. 12–end	Luke 1. 57–80
31	W	At Evening Prayer, the readings for the Eve of All Saints are used. At other services, the following readings are used:	
		Baruch ch. 5 or Hag. 1. 1–11	Mark 1. 1–11

November 2018

Date		Old Testament	New Testament
1	Th	ALL SAINTS' DAY	
		or, where All Saints' Day is celebrated on Sunday 4 November:	
		Isa. ch. 35	Matt. 11. 2–19
2	F	2 Sam. 11. 1–17	Matt. 14. 1–12
3	Sa	Isa. 43. 15–21	Acts 19. 1–10
4	S	THE FOURTH SUNDAY BEFORE ADVENT	
5	M	Esther 3. 1–11; 4. 7–17	Matt. 18. 1–10
6	Tu	Ezek. 18. 21–end	Matt. 18. 12–20
7	W	Prov. 3. 27–end	Matt. 18. 21–end
8	Th	Exod. 23. 1–9	Matt. 19. 1–15
9	F	Prov. 3. 13–18	Matt. 19. 16–end
10	Sa	Deut. 28. 1–6	Matt. 20. 1–16
11	S	THE THIRD SUNDAY BEFORE ADVENT	
12	M	Isa. 40. 21–end	Rom. 11. 25–end
13	Tu	Ezek. 34. 20–end	John 10. 1–18
14	W	Lev. 26. 3–13	Titus 2. 1–10
15	Th	Hos. 6. 1–6	Matt. 9. 9–13
16	F	Mal. ch. 4	John 4. 5–26
17	Sa	Mic. 6. 6–8	Col. 3. 12–17
18	S	THE SECOND SUNDAY BEFORE ADVENT	
19	M	Mic. 7. 1–7	Matt. 10. 24–39
20	Tu	Hab. 3. 1–19a	I Cor. 4. 9–16
21	W	Zech. 8. 1–13	Mark 13. 3–8
22	Th	Zech. 10. 6–end	I Pet. 5. 1–11

Date		Old Testament	New Testament
23	F	Mic. 4. 1–5	Luke 9. 28–36
24	Sa	At Evening Prayer, the readings for the Eve of Christ the King are used. At other services, the following readings are used:	
		Exod. 16. 1–21	John 6. 3–15
25	S	CHRIST THE KING (The Sunday next before Advent)	
26	M	Jer. 30. 1–3, 10–17	Rom. 12. 9–21
27	Tu	Jer. 30. 18–24	John 10. 22–30
28	W	Jer. 31. 1–9	Matt. 15. 21–31
29	Th	Jer. 31. 10–17	Matt. 16. 13–end
30	F	ANDREW	

December 2018

Date		Old Testament	New Testament
1	Sa	Isa. 51.17 – 52.2	Eph. 5. 1–20
2	S	THE FIRST SUNDAY OF ADVENT	
3	M	Mal. 3. 1–6	Matt. 3. 1–6
4	Tu	Zeph. 3. 14–end	I Thess. 4. 13–end
5	W	Isa. 65.17 – 66.2	Matt. 24. 1–14
6	Th	Mic. 5. 2–5a	John 3. 16–21
7	F	Isa. 66. 18–end	Luke 13. 22–30
8	Sa	Mic. 7. 8–15	Rom. 15.30 – 16.7, 25–end
9	S	THE SECOND SUNDAY OF ADVENT	
10	M	Jer. 7. 1–11	Phil. 4. 4–9
11	Tu	Dan. 7. 9–14	Matt. 24. 15–28
12	W	Amos 9. 11–end	Rom. 13. 8–14
13	Th	Jer. 23. 5–8	Mark 11. 1–11
14	F	Jer. 33. 14–22	Luke 21. 25–36
15	Sa	Zech. 14. 4–11	Rev. 22. 1–7
16	S	THE THIRD SUNDAY OF ADVENT	
17	M	Ecclus. 24. 1–9 or Prov. 8. 22–31	I Cor. 2. 1–13
18	Tu	Exod. 3. 1–6	Acts 7. 20–36
19	W	Isa. 11. 1–9	Rom. 15. 7–13
20	Th	Isa. 22. 21–23	Rev. 3. 7–13
21	F	Num. 24. 15b–19	Rev. 22. 10–21
22	Sa	Jer. 30. 7–11a	Acts 4. 1–12
23	S	THE FOURTH SUNDAY OF ADVENT	
24	M	At Evening Prayer, the readings for Christmas Eve are used. At other services, the following readings are used:	
		Isa. 29. 13–18	I John 4. 7–16
25	Tu	CHRISTMAS DAY	
26	W	STEPHEN	
27	Th	JOHN THE EVANGELIST	
28	F	THE HOLY INNOCENTS	
29	Sa	Mic. 1. 1–4; 2. 12–13	Luke 2. 1–7
30	S	THE FIRST SUNDAY OF CHRISTMAS	
31	M	Eccles. 3. 1–13	Rev. 21. 1–8

CALENDAR 2018

JANUARY
Su		7 B	14 E^2	21 E^3	28 E^4
M	1	8	15	22	29
Tu	2	9	16	23	30
W	3	10	17	24	31
Th	4	11	18	25	
F	5	12	19	26	
Sa	6 E	13	20	27	

FEBRUARY
Su		4 L^{-2}	11 L^{-1}	18 L^1	25 L^2
M		5	12	19	26
Tu		6	13	20	27
W		7	14 A	21	28
Th	1	8	15	22	
F	2 Pr	9	16	23	
Sa	3	10	17	24	

MARCH
Su		4 L^3	11 L^4	18 L^5	25 P
M		5	12	19	26
Tu		6	13	20	27
W		7	14	21	28
Th	1	8	15	22	29 M
F	2	9	16	23	30 G
Sa	3	10	17	24	31

APRIL
Su	1 E	8 E^2	15 E^3	22 E^4	29 E^5
M	2	9 An	16	23	30
Tu	3	10	17	24	
W	4	11	18	25	
Th	5	12	19	26	
F	6	13	20	27	
Sa	7	14	21	28	

MAY
Su		6 E^6	13 E^7	20 W	27 T
M		7	14	21	28
Tu	1	8	15	22	29
W	2	9	16	23	30
Th	3	10 A	17	24	31
F	4	11	18	25	
Sa	5	12	19	26	

JUNE
Su		3 T^1	10 T^2	17 T^3	24 T^4
M		4	11	18	25
Tu		5	12	19	26
W		6	13	20	27
Th		7	14	21	28
F	1	8	15	22	29
Sa	2	9	16	23	30

JULY
Su	1 T^5	8 T^6	15 T^7	22 T^8	29 T^9
M	2	9	16	23	30
Tu	3	10	17	24	31
W	4	11	18	25	
Th	5	12	19	26	
F	6	13	20	27	
Sa	7	14	21	28	

AUGUST
Su		5 T^{10}	12 T^{11}	19 T^{12}	26 T^{13}
M		6	13	20	27
Tu		7	14	21	28
W	1	8	15	22	29
Th	2	9	16	23	30
F	3	10	17	24	31
Sa	4	11	18	25	

SEPTEMBER
Su		2 T^{14}	9 T^{15}	16 T^{16}	23 T^{17}	30 T^{18}
M		3	10	17	24	
Tu		4	11	18	25	
W		5	12	19	26	
Th		6	13	20	27	
F		7	14	21	28	
Sa	1	8	15	22	29	

OCTOBER
Su		7 T^{19}	14 T^{20}	21 T^{21}	28 T^{-}
M	1	8	15	22	29
Tu	2	9	16	23	30
W	3	10	17	24	31
Th	4	11	18	25	
F	5	12	19	26	
Sa	6	13	20	27	

NOVEMBER
Su		4 A^{-4}	11 A^{-3}	18 A^{-2}	25 A^{-1}
M		5	12	19	26
Tu		6	13	20	27
W		7	14	21	28
Th	1 AS	8	15	22	29
F	2	9	16	23	30
Sa	3	10	17	24	

DECEMBER
Su		2 A	9 A^2	16 A^3	23 A^4	30 X^1
M		3	10	17	24	31
Tu		4	11	18	25 X	
W		5	12	19	26	
Th		6	13	20	27	
F		7	14	21	28	
Sa	1	8	15	22	29	

CALENDAR 2019

JANUARY
Su		6 E	13 B	20 E^2	27 E^3
M		7	14	21	28
Tu	1	8	15	22	29
W	2	9	16	23	30
Th	3	10	17	24	31
F	4	11	18	25	
Sa	5	12	19	26	

FEBRUARY
Su		3 L^{-5}	10 L^{-4}	17 L^{-3}	24 L^{-2}
M		4	11	18	25
Tu		5	12	19	26
W		6	13	20	27
Th		7	14	21	28
F	1	8	15	22	
Sa	2 Pr	9	16	23	

MARCH
Su		3 L^{-1}	10 L^1	17 L^2	24 L^3	31 L^4
M		4	11	18	25 An
Tu		5	12	19	26
W		6 A	13	20	27
Th		7	14	21	28
F	1	8	15	22	29
Sa	2	9	16	23	30

APRIL
Su		7 L^5	14 P	21 E	28 E^2
M	1	8	15	22	29
Tu	2	9	16	23	30
W	3	10	17	24	
Th	4	11	18 M	25	
F	5	12	19 G	26	
Sa	6	13	20	27	

MAY
Su		5 E^3	12 E^4	19 E^5	26 E^6
M		6	13	20	27
Tu		7	14	21	28
W	1	8	15	22	29
Th	2	9	16	23	30
F	3	10	17	24	31
Sa	4	11	18	25	

JUNE
Su		2 E^7	9 W	16 T	23 T^1	30 T^2
M		3	10	17	24
Tu		4	11	18	25
W		5	12	19	26
Th		6	13	20	27
F		7	14	21	28
Sa	1	8	15	22	29

JULY
Su		7 T^3	14 T^4	21 T^5	28 T^6
M	1	8	15	22	29
Tu	2	9	16	23	30
W	3	10	17	24	31
Th	4	11	18	25	
F	5	12	19	26	
Sa	6	13	20	27	

AUGUST
Su		4 T^7	11 T^8	18 T^9	25 T^{10}
M		5	12	19	26
Tu		6	13	20	27
W		7	14	21	28
Th	1	8	15	22	29
F	2	9	16	23	30
Sa	3	10	17	24	31

SEPTEMBER
Su	1 T^{11}	8 T^{12}	15 T^{13}	22 T^{14}	29 T^{15}	
M	2	9	16	23	30	
Tu	3	10	17	24		
W	4	11	18	25		
Th	5	12	19	26		
F	6	13	20	27		
Sa	7	14	21	28		

OCTOBER
Su		6 T^{16}	13 T^{17}	20 T^{18}	27 T^{-}
M		7	14	21	28
Tu	1	8	15	22	29
W	2	9	16	23	30
Th	3	10	17	24	31
F	4	11	18	25	
Sa	5	12	19	26	

NOVEMBER
Su		3 A^{-4}	10 A^{-3}	17 A^{-2}	24 A^{-1}
M		4	11	18	25
Tu		5	12	19	26
W		6	13	20	27
Th		7	14	21	28
F	1 AS	8	15	22	29
Sa	2	9	16	23	30

DECEMBER
Su	1 A	8 A^2	15 A^3	22 A^4	29 X^1
M	2	9	16	23	30
Tu	3	10	17	24	31
W	4	11	18	25 X	
Th	5	12	19	26	
F	6	13	20	27	
Sa	7	14	21	28	